Trusting Grace
The Journey from Fear to Love

J. Claude Huguley

© 2022
Published in the United States by Nurturing Faith Inc., Macon Ga.
Nurturing Faith is a book imprint of Good Faith Media (www.goodfaithmedia.org).

Library of Congress Cataloging-in-Publication Data is available.

ISBN: #978-1-63528-175-0
All rights reserved. Printed in the United States of America.

All scripture citations are taken from the New Revised Standard Version (NRSV) unless otherwise indicated.

"In this important volume, J. Claude Huguley brings thirty years of experience as a hospital chaplain to bear on insights for confronting life's traumas in ways that move through fear and insecurity to a spirituality shaped by love and grace. Using his own Christian commitments as illustration, Huguley offers creative spiritual guidance that explores the breadth, benefits, and possibilities of inner transformation. It could not be more timely."

—**Bill J. Leonard**
Professor of Divinity Emeritus
Wake Forest University

"Claude Huguley reminds us that a spiritual life is much more than an intellectual ascent to a set of beliefs. He describes a way of living with wholeness and authenticity that leads to fulfillment and depth of life. While he writes with references to Christian scripture, he captures a broadly applicable spiritual truth that profoundly reflects the human experience. The application of 1 John 4:18 ('perfect love casts out fear'), which forms the foundation of this book, provides opportunity for reflection on our relationship with ourselves and others and presents solid psychological principles through a spiritual lens that is accessible and not lost in overly spiritualized or technical jargon. I will be recommending this book to clients who are in need of this universal message of the power of love and grace."

—**Chris O'Rear**
Licensed Clinical Pastoral Therapist
Nashville, Tennessee

"In the pages of *Trusting Grace: The Journey from Fear to Love*, J. Claude Huguley offers the reader a biblically grounded, cognitive and behavioral analysis of destructive fear, its antecedents, and how we can journey onward by tapping into God's healing love. Huguley writes from his thirty-plus years of experience as a hospital chaplain in walking alongside people in the trauma and drama of life as they seek to name their experiences and review the relationships within their world. He reminds us that 'being human is an amazing gift' and as human beings we are invited to follow the lead of our Creator 'in a dance of giving, receiving, and giving again in trust.' He illustrates this in the healing and proactive responses of trust-filled submission, transparent honesty, grateful giving, and sacrificial service. Grace is the currency of love throughout. I invite you to read slowly, reflect deeply, and apply these principles liberally."

—**Gerry Hutchinson**
Retired Endorser for Chaplains and Pastoral Counselors
Cooperative Baptist Fellowship

"In our current season of overwhelming chaos and distress, *Trusting Grace* is gift for all who are seeking to make sense of the world. Claude Huguley, a thirty-year hospital chaplain, names clearly the fears that often consume us and speaks to those fears through spiritual wisdom found in a wide array of sources. His use of reflection questions and windows into scripture is an invitation to spiritual companionship for people of all faith traditions. This book is especially important for those who have been disappointed or disillusioned by faith leaders, religious institutions, and toxic traditions. *Trusting Grace* provides space and encouragement for those needing to reimagine their faith and/or find new purpose in life."

—**Pam Durso**
President, Central Seminary
Shawnee, Kansas

"The acquisition of expertise requires practice, lots of it. Informed sources suggest a minimum of 10,000 hours of concentrated repetition is needed to attain the highest level of performance. Claude Huguley has been a hospital chaplain for thirty years. Daily he has ministered to countless individuals and their families experiencing a crisis of health. Meeting these individuals in the complex crucible of a hospital setting, Claude has encountered a full range of human emotion. In *Trusting Grace*, he draws from this reservoir of pastoral care experience and speaks with expertise on the emotion of fear. As a hospital chaplain, Claude has observed closely an intense concentration of two layers of fear. One is the fear of being hurt, experiencing pain. The second is the underlying fear of death. As Virgil guided Dante through the inferno, Claude has accompanied many a stranger in a journey from fear to love. In *Trusting Grace*, he sets out to tell the story of the indefatigable power of grace to transform human lives. I am of the opinion that he writes as an expert."

—**Steven Meriwether**
Pastor, Immanuel Baptist Church
Nashville, Tennessee

Contents

Preface vii

Chapter 1: The Pathway from Giftedness to Fear
    Initial Gifts 1
    Limiting Gifts 5
    Disrespecting Limits 9
    Questions for Reflection 10
    The Parable of the Good Samaritan 10

Chapter 2: Turning the Gift of Limited Security into Dominating Fear
    Avoiding Awareness of Vulnerability 13
    Getting on the Treadmill 15
    Early Steps into Dominating Fear 16
    Tearing Down Others and Exploiting Their Vulnerabilities 18
    Questions for Reflection 22
    The Parable of a Rich Man 22

Chapter 3: Turning the Gift of Limited Resources into Grasping Fear
    Pursuing Possessions 25
    Recognizing Gratitude 28
    Grasping Expressions of Fear 30
    Questions for Reflection 34
    The Hazards of Public "Righteousness" 34

Chapter 4: Turning the Gift of Limited Knowledge into Lying Fear
    The Dance of Imagination and Knowledge 37
    Challenges Within This Collaborating Dance 39
    Hiding with Lying Fear 42
    Questions for Reflection 47
    The Story of Human Creation and Fall 48

Chapter 5: Turning the Gift of Limited Choice into Controlling Fear
    Searching for Control 51
    Strategies for Internal Control 52
    Seeking External Control and Finding a "god" of Fear 55
    Questions for Reflection 59
    The Parable of Two Lost Sons 60

Chapter 6: Being Found by the Giver of Love
    Being Found by LOVE 63
    Describing LOVE (Part 1) 64

Some Healing LOVE Opposites 67
Describing LOVE (Part 2) 70
Grace 72
Grumbling about Grace 74
Responding to LOVE 75
Questions for Reflection 81
The Philippian Hymn 81

Chapter 7: Transforming Controlling Fear with Submitting Love
Trusting Submissiveness 83
The Fruit of Submitting Love 86
Letting Be 88
Questions for Reflection 92
A Psalm of Confession 93

Chapter 8: Transforming Lying Fear with Revealing Love
Trusting Grace 95
Limiting Grace 96
Revealing with Trust 98
Practicing Revealing Love 100
Questions for Reflection 103
A Parable of Forgiveness 103

Chapter 9: Transforming Grasping Fear with Giving Love
Recognizing Giftedness 107
Unleashing Gratitude 109
Giving Love 111
Countering Unforgiveness 113
Questions for Reflection 116
Redefining "Greatness" 117

Chapter 10: Transforming Dominating Fear with Serving Love
Choosing Vulnerability 119
Serving Love 122
Seeing and Responding Differently 124
Questions for Reflection 128

Conclusion
When We Lose Our Way—Again 129
Simon Peter and Restoring Grace 129
Trusting Grace and LOVE for Life's Journey 131

Acknowledgments 133

Preface

"There is no fear in love, but perfect love casts out fear."
(1 John 4:18a)

According to a kernel of wisdom commonly passed along in the 12-Step recovery community, "There are two things to remember about God: First, 'there *is* a God'; second, '*I* am not God.'" These "two things" are simple and profound, but easily forgotten. Forgetting them has consequences. It is like going skydiving and not remembering to strap on a parachute. This forgetting not only sets in motion a bad ending, but also fills remaining time with fear.

I believe our society—and many of us as individuals—have forgotten these "two things." We are now consumed in fear. Fear changes what we see, how we see, and what we value. It changes us and changes our relationships in distortive and destructive ways.

Fear takes many forms. Our fear may be about personal security. The twenty-four-hour news cycle is filled with stories of natural disasters, wars, and violent crimes that highlight human vulnerability. These fascinate and threaten. It is fascinating when we observe dreaded events through the safer eye of the camera; it is threatening when we realize these could happen to us or those we love.

Our fear may show as we worry about our things. Our society enjoys more goods, services, and conveniences than previous generations would have dreamed possible. Does this relative abundance make us content? Do we feel closer to having "enough"? Not hardly. The more we have, the more we want, and the less satisfied and secure we feel. Our fear makes us guard what we have and keep seeking more.

Anxieties about personal image fuel fear. Our society fixates on the lives of celebrities. These "stars" from Hollywood, sports, politics, business, and even religion are often held up as standards for comparison. From one extreme, we may feel we never measure up; from the other extreme, we may feel superior because "at least I'm not like *them*." All along this continuum, this celebrity standard points us toward presenting ourselves (and even seeing ourselves) as we would like to appear, rather than as the people we truly are.

Fear can also seep into our understanding of God. How many of us have internalized a picture of the divine as a great "boogie man," constantly waiting to catch us in a fault so punishment can be unleashed? The coercive power in this image may motivate in the moment but robs us of any sense of safety, seeding the fruits of distrust and conflict on a personal and worldwide scale.

All these sources of fear create a need for control. Forgetting the mantra that "I am not God," we try to create our own safety by exercising control over the world around us. Dictating, objectifying, dominating, grasping, guarding, hiding, lying—using these and all their derivatives, we attempt to soothe our fear. With time, these strategies fail and our relationships suffer. We create more fear for ourselves, adding to the fear in the world. Is there a better way?

My own perspectives about fear and potentials for transformation have been shaped by experience serving as a hospital chaplain for more than thirty years. As "generic" ministers, hospital chaplains walk alongside anyone who would desire help in making meaning and sense of the world. It matters little whether that individual claims a traditional faith understanding or would rather not use the language of any faith. For me, the wisdom in spiritual understanding comes from many sources. Each of us can benefit from the varying insights we discover while traveling on our own journey of meaning. The key question would seem to be: "Does this insight help me name and understand my own experience and the relationships within my world?"

If so, we are free to incorporate the insight into our ongoing searches for meaning. If not, we are free to discard any ideas we may find questionable, unusable, or wrong. We may also choose to withhold final judgment for now and see where our understanding takes us.

In this book, I will approach spirituality and "meaning making" from this more open-ended stance, while making use of stories and teachings that come from my own Christian tradition. I hope my particular framing of them will assist both Christians and any other seekers of meaning in their individual life journeys.

Chapters 1–5 will unmask destructive fear—its origins, its reach, and the many ways it undermines and destroys individual relationships and sabotages community. Exposing fear disarms its coercive power, freeing us. Chapters 6–10 invite us into a new way of living, realigning our lives with *LOVE** and allowing the gifts of grace to transform destructive expressions of fear into personal healing and life-giving community. I hope readers will join with me, trusting grace for the journey.

---

*I use LOVE (all caps) to denote the indescribable love characterizing and coming from the Creator. I use love (lower case) to describe the human love that sometimes mirrors LOVE. For the purpose of emphasis, key word combinations having specific meaning are italicized in initial references.

Chapter 1
The Pathway from Giftedness to Fear

Initial Gifts

Being human is an amazing gift! How easily and often we overlook this truth. None of us came into this world by our own choice or doing. We received life by the actions of others, and from the beginning we depended on the care of others to sustain our lives. While each of us might claim this life as our own, it has never been completely our own; our lives continually and interdependently intersect with the lives of others.

We each began as a single cell. From this cell came billions and billions of individual specialized cells. Every cell carries out specific functions to meet the needs of the body as a whole as each supports the other individual cells that make up the body. This human body can live a century and beyond, but the lifespan of individual cells in our body is much shorter. Throughout our lifetime, whenever an individual cell is injured, wears out, or dies, these old cells are replaced with new and identical specialized cells that carry on their function. Carrying a copy of the genetic code, each new cell "knows" what to do and how to do it. Coordinating with other cells in the body, the cell "knows" when to grow and replicate, when to slow its growth, and when to die. With amazing complexity and coordination, our living is sustained each day.

A distinguishing characteristic of our humanity is our consciousness—we are aware that we are. We can think, and think about our thinking. We can remember what has gone before, imagine what may be in the future, and observe and ponder what is happening now. Our cognitive skills change us and change the world around us.

Cognitive awareness is a gift we receive. It begins with the potential for consciousness we have at conception, but its development depends upon the contributions of others. Starting out incapable of caring for ourselves, we watch, hear, and learn from those who care for us, talk to us, and value us. Our language skills grow from simple words to abstract reasoning, and our consciousness and cognitive capacity emerge. All of this requires assistance. We are given, we receive, and then we choose what we do with each gift.

This interdependence we share nourishes human life and relationships. Those who gave to us were once receivers themselves and chose to give to us. Having received, we have the opportunity to give to the generations that follow us and to give back to those who nurtured us.

A corresponding interdependence works within each of us with our own bodies. In my consciousness, I have the perception of command and control, but I actually have little understanding of the inner workings of my own body. I may be directing the movements of my body, the focus of my observations, and the content of my thinking, but I do all this with little conscious awareness of the complex cellular and subcellular processes that make these actions possible. Throughout each day my heart rate, breathing, digestion, blood pressure, waste removal, body temperature, and countless other life-dependent body functions are continually monitored and maintained as my body adapts to conditions inside and outside my body. In each moment, billions of simultaneous interactions are coordinated with little or no input from my conscious mind. My very awareness itself depends upon this same process.

As humans, we each share this common experience. Scientists who study these individual biological and chemical processes in greater detail discover that each layer understood only uncovers new layers of more intricate complexity. Being human, at its core, is an amazing gift that defies our best efforts to explain it.

> Being human is an amazing gift that defies our best efforts to explain it.

For me, recognizing the giftedness of human life prompts questions: How did this life-sustaining process of giving, receiving, and giving again get started? If life *is* a gift, is it reasonable to speculate about the possibility of a Giver behind the gift—a Creator—One who makes the gift of life possible? Religious teachings are frequently rooted in this possibility, and many religions assume a Source beyond us.

Much as I have little conscious connection to the inner workings of my own body, any connection to a higher power relies on something beyond what can be directly observed and explained by our conscious minds. Commonly, we use the word "faith" to describe this kind of "seeing." At its best, faith respects the tools of cognitive reasoning and careful observation. Faith also sees beyond the explainable and observable.

Being a gift that offers a different way of "seeing," faith enables us to discern meaning and direction in the midst of the often confusing and contradictory circumstances of living. As a hospital chaplain, I have been privileged to listen as others have fleshed out their faith, seeking to make sense in the face of life challenges. I have found that faith broadens perspective, offering expanded opportunities and new gifts.

Faith, like language, is learned from the people around us. It reflects a shared understanding about values and questions of meaning. The faith we learn from others is often expressed in stories, and these stories of faith provide answers to questions—about human origins, boundaries of appropriate human behavior, and desired relationships with a higher power. Listening to the stories of faith, we can connect our own life experiences to the wider stories that have impacted past generations. These older faith stories can then help us frame the way we see and interpret our current understanding.

The substance of faith need not be limited to these familiar stories and their long-held interpretations. Just as we can move beyond the language of our birth and learn new languages, we can also expand the reaches of our faith understanding beyond our original group and include new experiences and modes of expressing ideas. Doing this can enrich and enhance our living, but we would still be wise to maintain respect for the collected wisdom of previous generations. Listening and learning from people of faith who have "seen" before us, we stand on their shoulders with opportunity for seeing further or better understanding what their faith might reveal.

What has been "seen" by people of faith in past generations? Coming from a Judeo-Christian tradition, I begin with a faith story from the first chapter of Genesis. Here we find the story of a Creator God whose very nature is giving. This giving Creator brings all things into being and calls the creation "good." The finishing gift of this giving God is creating beings in the likeness of God's own self and entrusting the rest of creation into their care.

> Then God said, "Let us make humankind in our image, according to our likeness; and let them have dominion over the fish of the sea, and over the birds of the air, and over the cattle, and over all the wild animals of the earth, and over every creeping thing that creeps upon the earth."
>
> So God created humankind in his image, in the image of God he created them; male and female he created them.
>
> God blessed them, and God said to them, "Be fruitful and multiply, and fill the earth and subdue it; and have dominion over the fish of the sea and over the birds of the air and over every living thing that moves upon the earth." God said, "See, I have given you every plant yielding seed that is upon the face of all the earth, and every tree with seed in its fruit; you shall have them for food. And to every beast of the earth, and to every bird of the air, and to everything that creeps on the earth, everything that has the breath of life, I have given every green plant for food." And it was so. God saw everything that he had made, and indeed, it was very good. (Gen. 1:26-31a)

The Creator gives a three-part gift to humanity: the likeness of God, the blessing of fruitfulness, and authority over the rest of creation. With each gift, the Creator demonstrates trust. Each is a trust-filled gift of capacity and possibility: fulfillment depends on humanity's recognition of the gifts and the willingness to develop and actualize them.

> The Creator gives a three-part gift to humanity: the likeness of God, the blessing of fruitfulness, and authority over the rest of creation.

As an all-too-familiar story, we can easily overlook some profound insights into the Creator's values. In giving these open-ended gifts, the Creator is practicing vulnerability, giving up control over how each capacity is developed and used. Giving up control is the ultimate demonstration of trust, but clearly is the intention of the Creator. This is no accident. According to the story, the Creator sees the finished product and declares it "very good." This vulnerable and trusting Creator God is modeling eternal values and inviting the whole of humanity to join in vulnerability and trust.

The Creator's invitation recognizes a human capacity that sets us apart from the rest of creation—the power to make choices. With this capacity, we human creatures reflect our greater kinship with the Creator and our unique distinction from the rest of creation. Everything else that is non-human functions according to natural laws and programmed instincts that merely sense and react to the environment.

When the aforementioned gift of conscious awareness is combined with another gift—the gift of imagination—the combination gives birth to our distinctive choice-making capacity. Imagination, growing out of our conscious awareness, enables us to "see" things that are not physically present and to visualize not only ourselves but also the world around us from differing perspectives. Our imagination lets us test out new roles and consider possibilities without being bound by the limits of our physical world. With imagination, we enlarge our world. Our creative imaginations formulate real alternatives from which we can choose.

Power to make choices is only a capacity until we actually start choosing. At that moment of first choice, we express both the fullness of our humanity and our likeness to the Creator. Our exercising of decisional willpower starts even before we are toddlers (as our caregivers could attest.) These earliest choices unleash all the future possibilities and choices that can follow.

The development of decisional willpower makes possible a new dimension of human relating: trust. Following the model of the Creator who has given with trust, we, the human creation can choose to receive and then give back with trust. Giving back with trust is based in the trusting confidence that our need will continue to be supplied. This element of trust expands our understanding of the originating faith story. The story is not just about giving, receiving, and giving again; it is about giving, receiving, and giving again with trust. Giving and trust go together. They express both the will and the intention of the Creator.

> Giving and trust express both the will and the intention of the Creator.

The Creator exercises trust in humanity by inviting each of us to participate in the blessing of fruitfulness. The Creator's vision of fruitfulness is not merely growing in number; it is fulfilling—living out—the totality of being made in the image of the Creator. Fulfillment is no small task. Acquiring knowledge, developing self-awareness, and employing imagination are required if we are to formulate alternatives and make decisions. We determine and we choose the level of our fruitfulness. Will our human choices reflect trust in the Creator and align with the Creator's values? The trusting Creator has not predetermined our choices. We are free to affirm or deviate from the will of the Creator. Whether our choices result in fruitfulness or fruitlessness, the Creator blesses us with the freedom of choosing. The Creator is choosing trust.

In a third act of trust, the Creator gives humanity the opportunity to exercise Creator-sanctioned authority—rule—in relation to the rest of creation. Having already given up control over the choices of humans, the Creator extends that trust by giving humanity ruling authority with all its potential hopes and risks. Once again, we as humans are presented with a fundamental choice. How will this rule be exercised? Will it mimic the trust-filled path of giving, receiving, and giving again, or will it deviate from the Creator's example and choose a different path?

I have moments when I recognize the truly amazing gifts I have received in being human—being alive, being loved, having awareness and imagination, having the capacity to learn, to grow, to interact, and to choose. In these moments, this faith story from Genesis feels true and life-giving in its description of a trusting and giving Creator and my own place in the creation. The story makes sense of the interdependence we humans share with the creation on every level (whether we acknowledge it or not.)

I also see the world in which we live. The faith story's focus upon radical giving and vulnerable trust seems so counter to the distrust and "look out for number one" mentality that often appears to guide our everyday experience. Is the faith story hopelessly naïve, or is there a reasonable explanation for how things got sidetracked? Is there a way I, and others like me, can rejoin this "dance" of giving, receiving, and giving again with trust?

Limiting Gifts

So far, I have identified gifts that speak to human potential—what can happen if we live to the fullest of our possibilities. This is only part of the picture. We humans also live in a world that subjects us to limitations and requires ongoing navigation among these limits. The gifts of conscious awareness, imagination, and choice-making capacity are constrained by countless limits.

Some constraints are physical. We are limited by the force of gravity and must function within the laws of physics. This is what makes jumping out of an airplane without a parachute problematic. Other physical constraints result from the ever-present bodily requirements for sustaining life—oxygen, proper nutrition, hydration, rest, and sufficient clothing and shelter to protect from the elements.

Some constraints are limits of space and time. I can only be physically present in one place at a time; I can only act in this moment. My choice to do something in this place at this time excludes the possibility of being in other places and doing other things at the same moment. Coordinating calendars with others may mean modifying original choices and adjusting my plans to account for the limiting wishes of other people.

The limitations of our own bodies constrain us. Age, physical size, strength, and our overall health—and our perception of these—can limit what we are able to do. In the spring of our lives our physical capabilities grow with the maturing of our bodies; these diminish as we move through the seasons of our lifespan. This decline becomes ever more limiting as we move toward death, the final limitation. As a chaplain, I well understand that an awareness of our own mortality is always in the background, reminding us that someday we will no longer have the option of choosing. Until then, limits are shaping our living and our choices.

Limitations may feel like burdens or obstacles, but they are still gifts. Without limits, we would lack focus in our choices. Limitations around bodily needs prompt us to address those needs; limitations within our relationships encourage us to develop more cooperative interactions that could expand our options. Even the prospect of our own mortality is a gift. In my role as chaplain, I have been at the bedside of many patients who are facing a life-limiting illness. Those living with a terminal diagnosis often have more clarity about what is truly important than those who carry the perception of unlimited time. The gnawing awareness of limited time brings keener focus and direction. Loose ends are tied up, needed expressions of love are exchanged, reconciliation happens, and valuable time is shared.

> Limitations may feel like burdens or obstacles, but they are still gifts.

Recognizing this giftedness within limits prompts us to look again at the faith story in Genesis of the Creator God who gives with trust. Limits are built into this creation that the Creator labeled "very good." These constraints provide boundaries that allow humanity to join together in a dance of giving, receiving, and giving again with trust. When viewed through this life-expanding lens, our limits are not confining; they free us to live in the fullness of the Creator's intention.

How might we describe these limits that humanity receives as gifts? I infer from observation four broad categories of limitation: the gift of limited security, the gift of limited resources, the gift of limited knowledge, and the gift of limited choice. Each of these limiting gifts supports the giving, receiving, and giving again intended by the Creator.

Limited security may be the most obvious limit we humans face. Some of the physical limitations already described remind us that our bodies are vulnerable to aging, disease, natural forces, and the harmful choices of others. There may be no absolute security from harm, and mortality still awaits us all, but the vulnerability exposed by limited security remains a gift. This vulnerability activates an alertness and respect for the outside world that helps us avoid harm individually. It simultaneously prompts reaching out to those around us and interdependently supporting the greater safety of our community.

Limited resources promote thoughtful stewardship, helping us distinguish between mere wants and genuine needs, between "now" and "not yet." The Creator has collectively given humanity the resources and skills we need; we are far more limited individually. In the Creator's intended economy of giving, receiving, and giving again with trust, we are prompted to share resources, wait our turn, and "look not to your own interests, but to the interest of others" (Phil. 2:4). Working cooperatively, we can pool our skills and resources, meeting the larger needs for food, medical care, shelter, and all other needs necessary for sustaining meaningful life.

If I think I know everything, I have little incentive to learn or grow. *Limited knowledge* stokes curiosity and promotes a search for knowledge and truth on an individual and global scale. When I expand my personal knowledge, I grow my opportunities and choices, learning humility from what is yet unknown. On the global scale, this gift of limited knowledge teaches wider collaboration. Working together, we know more and learn more. In the diversity of our differences, we discover new ways of knowing from one another, expanding the scope of human understanding together. The "dance" of giving, receiving, and giving again with trust creates new learning and possibility.

Within the boundaries of truth, human knowledge thrives. While we can reframe truth and observe it from differing vantage points, we cannot change truth to fit our desires. One obvious example of this is human mortality. Even as we expand the knowledge of medical treatments that may forestall death for days, weeks or years, these efforts are merely postponing the inevitable. We still will die. Changing the truth of human mortality is not an option.

Unfortunately, sorting out the truth is not always simple or obvious. How do we distinguish absolute truth from partial truth? If absolute truth is truth that rings true from any vantage point, how do we distinguish this from "truths" that ring true from many but not all perspectives? We humans (me included) are tempted to attach certainty to ideas and perceptions that only reflect a partial understanding. Admitting the limits of our personal knowledge helps us disarm the pride and temper the dogmatism that cuts off dialogue and a deeper search for understanding. The gift of limited knowledge teaches us to listen to the wider world.

Limited security, limited resources, and limited knowledge together give birth to the gift of *limited choice*. None of us have absolute control over our personal safety, world resources, or the management of truth. We have little control over the alternatives from which we choose or the choices others make. Despite this, working collaboratively with others expands choice—individually and collectively. Together we have more choice and more opportunity than any of us has in isolation. Prompting respect for others and promoting cooperative interaction, this gift of limited choice encourages community.

If these limits have the potential to bring the human community together, they can also draw us toward the Creator. Limits remind me that "I am not God" and my own need for a Source of security, resources, knowledge, and expanding choices beyond myself. The Creator's intended "dance" of giving, receiving, and giving again offers a consistent practice for building trust within the creation and with the Creator. Each gift of limitation makes these relationships possible.

> The Creator's intended "dance" of giving, receiving, and giving again offers a consistent practice for building trust within the creation and with the Creator.

Recognizing the giftedness in limits offers an orienting perspective on life for me. In reality, though, limitedness is also a given. We either accept reality, seeing the life-enhancing freedom of its boundaries, or we pay the consequences, spending our resources and knowledge in resistance. If we are choosing acceptance, how do we recognize our individual limitations in each situation? We exercise another gift: healthy and constructive fear.

Healthy fear alerts us to the presence of physical limits, prompting respect for them and promoting safety. It makes us careful when we climb a ladder or monitor the speed of our car. While less obvious, healthy fear alerts us to limits related to resources, knowledge, or choice. It prompts listening, valuing, and accounting for boundaries so we can live in trust and safety.

Healthy fear walks hand-in-hand with the gift of imagination. We produce healthy fear when our imagination is focused on understanding and respecting the particular limits constraining us. Working in concert with the gifts of awareness and imagination, healthy fear anticipates the possible dangerous consequences resulting from disrespecting a real limit. When we are crossing a busy street, healthy fear warns us of the imagined dangers so we cross carefully and safely. In similar fashion, healthy fear may warn us of the dangers of telling a lie as we imagine the potential harmful consequences of that telling.

Healthy fear only warns. It alerts us to the boundary or potential danger but does not determine what we do with the warning. Making that decision is our will. Our will

The Pathway from Giftedness to Fear

considers the warnings of healthy fear and chooses whether to listen to these prompts. If it so chooses, the will selects from the options supplied by the limit-respecting imagination and takes action.

Navigating through the limits of security, resources, knowledge, and choice is challenging. The collaboration of the gifts of awareness, imagination, and healthy fear provides direction. Together, these help us envision new ways of ensuring our safety, making use of our resources, and providing new vantage points for observing and understanding truth. They assist us in expanding the alternatives from which we can choose as we seek to stay on a life-giving path.

Disrespecting Limits

The collaboration of awareness and imagination results in healthy fear as long as respect for limits is maintained. What if our imagination is focused in a different direction, questioning the validity of real limits or discounting the consequences of violating them? Envisioning a world where limits do not exist or constraints do not bind is possible. Making use of this broader capacity, our imagination is able to see paths around real limits or the potential consequences attached to them.

Directing our imagination is our will. Our will can actively choose to steer the imagination toward understanding and respecting limits or toward defying and circumventing them. A third option is also available: passively allowing the imagination to pursue its own direction. Whether our will is making active or passive choices, these decisions can have far-reaching consequences.

An imagination focusing on understanding, respecting, and living within the constraints of real limits produces healthy and constructive fear. An imagination focusing on superseding or circumventing limits produces a different kind of fear: *destructive fear*. Unfortunately, the harmful effects of disrespecting limits and the destructive fear it is creating may not be immediately evident.

The harm comes from disturbing the Creator's life-giving harmony of giving, receiving, and giving again with trust. Trust is invaluable, but fragile and easily broken. I have learned that trust placed in that which is trustworthy invites further trust; in contrast, distrustfulness breeds more distrust. When I distrust the life-enhancing limits of the Creator, it undermines the very foundations of my trust. It is like cutting off the tree limb that is supporting my weight. Distrusting real limits while I am still trusting in the One who supplies the gift of those limits is just not possible.

This loss in trust is costly. Participating in the "dance" of giving, receiving, and giving again requires ongoing trust. If we distrust and resist real limits we are also undermining our basic trust that the Giver will resupply what we need to replace what we would be giving away. When we shut off our faucet of "giving again," we stop living out of the free flow of gift and stop the "dance."

> When we shut off our faucet of "giving again,"
> we stop living out of the free flow of gift and stop the "dance."

Stopping the "dance" changes us, changing the focus of our imaginations. No longer trusting the gifts of the Giver, we start envisioning ways we can selfishly meet our own needs—increasing our own power and shaping others and the world around us to our will. Following this distrustful course not only undercuts the basis of our own trust, but it also sabotages the trust others place in us. Trust, once lost, is hard to restore.

As this is happening, it may not seem so problematic. The sense of freedom, power, and control that comes from resisting or defying limits can be intoxicating—even as the momentary high from this is deceptive. But we are not toying with some peripheral or minor boundary; we are changing the orientation—the center—out of which we perceive and interact with the world.

We are moving out of seeing life as a gift and moving into seeing the world as subject to our demands. We are switching from grateful receiver to willful taker. We are exchanging the life-giving trust in the Giver for a life-sapping "trust" in our ability to obtain our own security, resources, knowledge, and choice. Finally, we are disregarding the fact that we are creatures and asserting that we can be gods, forgetting the maxim "there is a God and I am not God." This choice changes everything. Destructive fear is born.

Questions for Reflection

1. Which of the gifts of being human are you most grateful for and why?
2. How does the image of a giving Creator God who practices vulnerability and trust toward the creation align with what you have been taught about the Divine? How might this image shift your own faith perspective?
3. What limits are hardest to accept and why?
4. How have your relationships been impacted by a loss of trust? If trust was restored, how did this happen?

A Window from Scripture

The Parable of the Good Samaritan
(Luke 10:25-37)

Vulnerability is discomforting and scary. Valuing strength, independence, and self-sufficiency, we resist even the thought of being weak, dependent, or needy. A resistance to vulnerability even influences how we read and interpret familiar stories from scripture. In this story, most of us identify with the hero. We may overlook that Jesus encourages hearers to put themselves in the shoes of the robbed and vulnerable man.

> Just then a lawyer stood up to test Jesus. "Teacher," he said, "what must I do to inherit eternal life?" He said to him, "What is written in the law? What do you read there?" He answered, "You shall love the Lord your God with all your heart, and with all your soul, and with all your strength, and with all your mind; and your neighbor as yourself." And he said to him, "You have given the right answer; do this, and you will live."
>
> But wanting to justify himself, he asked Jesus, "And who is my neighbor?" Jesus replied, "A man was going down from Jerusalem to Jericho, and fell into the hands of robbers, who stripped him, beat him, and went away, leaving him half dead. Now by chance a priest was going down that road; and when he saw him, he passed by on the other side. So likewise a Levite, when he came to the place and saw him, passed by on the other side. But a Samaritan while traveling came near him; and when he saw him, he was moved with pity. He went to him and bandaged his wounds, having poured oil and wine on them. Then he put him on his own animal, brought him to an inn, and took care of him. The next day he took out two denarii, gave them to the innkeeper, and said, 'Take care of him; and when I come back, I will repay you whatever more you spend.' Which of these three, do you think, was a neighbor to the man who fell into the hands of the robbers?" He said, "The one who showed him mercy." Jesus said to him, "Go and do likewise."

This familiar story of Jesus, commonly known as the Parable of the Good Samaritan, tells the story of a man beset upon by robbers. Most interpreters rightly focus on the main point of the story—answering the question of the expert in the law that prompted the parable: "Who is my neighbor?"

Interpreters usually note the less-than-neighborly responses of the two outwardly religious authorities, the priest and the Levite, contrasting their inaction with the extraordinary generosity and compassion of the Samaritan. This unexpected hero was of a religion, race, and culture considered highly deficient and even hated by Jesus' hearers. With his masterful storytelling, Jesus dispels the prejudicial stereotyping limiting an understanding of "neighbor" while broadening both the definition of our neighbor and responsibilities to them.

Hearers and interpreters of the story often miss a subtle shift Jesus makes about "neighbor" in his question to the lawyer at the conclusion of the story. Note that Jesus does not ask, "Which of these three showed kindness to his neighbor?" This question would have identified the "neighbor" as the robbed and beaten man who needed mercy and assistance. Viewing the "neighbor" this way, the one who loved the neighbor could do so from a superior position—as the one with power helping the one in need. Seeing the neighbor from this position of power is appealing.

But Jesus turns the power relationships around with the question he does ask: "Which of these three, do you think, was a neighbor to the man who fell into the hands of the robbers?" Answering this actual question required taking on the vantage point of the robbed and beaten man. Lying half dead by the road, this desperate, needy, and vulnerable man had to look up to see who was a neighbor to him. Only from an awareness of his need could the true neighbor be identified.

This subtle but profound shift does not negate the common takeaway of the parable—that each of us has moral responsibility to assist those in need. Jesus' question just calls for more—recognizing that we are vulnerable and needy ourselves. We need a neighbor as much as others need us to be a neighbor to them. Loving our neighbor is to be mutual—a willingness to give, to receive, and to trust. Loving God, loving neighbor, and loving self becomes another expression of the dance of giving, receiving, and giving again with trust.

Jesus' actual question is prompting us to a much more profound and life-altering understanding of what it means to "love your neighbor as yourself." Yes, vulnerability is discomforting and scary. But vulnerability also unleashes love. Indeed, love flows most freely as neediness is opening space for it. Jesus is inviting us to see our neighbor's need while recognizing that we are needy too. This frees us to fully love our neighbor and ourselves. Being vulnerable may still be hard, but Jesus' story is planting seeds for a more fruitful way of living and loving.

Chapter 2
Turning the Gift of Limited Security into Dominating Fear

Avoiding Awareness of Vulnerability

Being human is an amazing gift! Accepting the vulnerability exposed by *limited security* supports the fullest expression of that gift—the dance of giving, receiving, and giving again with trust. But we can easily forget this and abandon the trust-filled "dance" when we are focusing on protecting ourselves from harm. Trust always contains an element of uncertainty—a leap of faith. Living vulnerable within the boundaries of healthy fear is hard. Doing our own securing and living as if we are unbound by real limits seems safer and more certain. It is not.

Any search for certainty in security is ultimately doomed to fail. Human vulnerability is plain to see. Earthquakes, floods, hurricanes, tornadoes, and other acts of nature highlight human vulnerability to the elements. A car wreck, a fire, an industrial accident, or just being "in the wrong place at the wrong time" can result in death or life-altering injuries. Violent death or injury can come from war or the random hostile act of another.

This non-exhaustive listing does not include vulnerabilities to sickness, economic setbacks, or insufficient food, water, and shelter. The totality of these vulnerabilities underscores the magnitude of human insecurity. No amount of vigilance or preparation provides absolute security or protection from harm. Limited security is the reality of our world.

While we might willfully acknowledge this truth of limited security in a global and absolute sense, it is quite another thing to grasp just how vulnerable we are in each moment. Carrying this awareness in every moment would overwhelm us. We tend to manage by burying this overwhelming insecurity below the surface of our consciousness. Using mental gymnastics, we intellectually acknowledge the facts while doing all we can to deny the full truth of our vulnerability.

I sometimes see examples of this in my interactions with patients and their families. They may tell their doctor they want the full picture of their health condition and prognosis, but only listen for the parts indicating a better outcome. They discount the more ominous elements, focusing on the strengths and personal attributes making a bad outcome unlikely.

I have learned not to stand in judgment; this strategy may be helping them cope with a harsh reality. Besides, none of us are immune to this tempting strategy of denial. Despite my training and experience, I can easily revert to it myself when something concerns my own health or the health of those closest to me. Acknowledging vulnerability is hard.

> Acknowledging vulnerability is hard.

Two nonrational assumptions energize denials of vulnerability. The first one asserts we can make ourselves secure by increasing our strength and power. Believing this sets us on a pursuit of anything we perceive might make us stronger and more powerful—especially in relation to those around us. Independence and self-sufficiency are the goal. We may seek better education or better relationships, more material possessions or prestige, healthier eating or exercise, or anything else (weapons included) offering a protective insulation from the vulnerabilities we fear.

Marketers and advertisers constantly exploit one or more of these in their appeals. Unfortunately, these seductive security-boosters rarely satisfy. Like the proverbial carrot on a stick just beyond our reach, this yearning for security-promising power continually entices us into seeking what we can never have. More strength and power cannot make us absolutely secure.

The second nonrational assumption tells us that greater vigilance can make us secure. Prudence and safe practices can help us avoid many dangers, but much that happens to us can never be anticipated. After undesirable things happen, we may question, "Could I have prevented this if I had been more vigilant and watchful?" This review sets us up for heightened vigilance. Focusing not just on our own experience, we may extend our angst outward to what we observe happening to our neighbors and learn through the media. "If it happened to them, might it not happen to me... and what might I do to protect myself and avoid it?" Although some untoward events might be prevented by greater vigilance, there is a cost. Linking our imagination with heightened vigilance can make the world feel ever more frightening and dangerous.

Coupling imagination with heightened vigilance creates another problem. It turns a critical spotlight on our fledgling efforts at growing our sources of personal power. More strength, better relationships, and more possessions are also sources of new vulnerability. Where might these fail us? How might these be taken from us or be used against us? As long as we are making these the hallmarks of our security, perceiving their vulnerability will be threatening. Spotlighting potential weaknesses undermines any increased security we might have received from enhancing our strength and power. Exposing this problem provides a troubling reminder: any source of strength is tenuous and always at risk of fading. The discomfort from this vulnerability does not lessen with awareness—it grows.

Getting on the Treadmill

Trying to bury conscious awareness of vulnerability puts us into an impossible and unsustainable bind. Pursuing an ever-growing, security-promising power and maintaining an ever-vigilant attention to threats is exhausting. Coping devolves into a mindless rush of constant busyness: a treadmill. This busyness clouds, numbs, and distracts us from seeing the true impact of all these pressures on our behaviors and attitudes. It is a treadmill of our own making, but eventually it carries us to relational destructiveness and hurt.

Much of what I am describing functions outside our conscious awareness. The mental gymnastics needed for hiding this hiddenness from ourselves leads us into ever expanding and intertwined layers of concealment. Just as an initial lie requires a widening web of lies to maintain credibility, so this burying of conscious awareness of vulnerability becomes more and more unstable. Maintaining our feeling of "security" requires ongoing self-deception. This creates its own threat of exposure, bringing new sources of vulnerability. What a mess!

Criticizing this strategy of denial and self-deception might be easy, but wisdom would suggest being kind in our assessment. This denial is not about being dishonest; it is about being scared. I remember standing at the bedside of a woman whose loved one had just died. The body was lifeless. The nurse told her he was dead. But with complete sincerity she looked at me and said, "He's not dead... he's just sleeping... he was sleeping just like this yesterday."

In that moment, the prospect of her loved one's death was so scary and overwhelming that she could not allow the harsh reality into her consciousness. Yes, her response was unusual and dramatic, but it illustrates the driving force underlying any efforts to bury conscious awareness of our vulnerability. We are scared. Recognizing the full reality of our vulnerability can just be too frightening. (An aside: A few minutes later this same woman felt safe enough to acknowledge her loved one's death and then began the real work of grieving.)

> Denial is not about being dishonest; it is about being scared.

If the actual vulnerabilities in our world are frightening, burying awareness of them only makes them more threatening. Self-deception requires energy, and this misplaced energy ramps up our aversion to vulnerability and exposure. Irrational actions and relationally destructive reactions often follow.

We cannot escape the vulnerability inherent in human limitation—individually or collectively. Limited security is reality and forces us to choose between two scary and undesirable options. One choice is facing the true reality of human insecurity and our vulnerability to harm. Accepting this reality, we use healthy fear as a guide to manage the real dangers we encounter. We face our anxieties directly, acting immediately while living with the insecurity. Exercising this choice has one sure consequence—a quick and certain path to instantaneous discomfort. After all, absolute security is never possible.

The other choice is staying on the treadmill—avoiding and denying the realities of human life. We maintain constant busyness, distracting and numbing our awareness of truth. During that moment, this second choice feels easier and safer, temporarily quieting our anxiety, appearing to make sense. Why live in the certainty of insecurity when we can imagine postponing vulnerability, shifting it to someone else or avoiding it all together?

In the short-term, this reality-avoidant strategy works. The problems emerge with the passing of time. Reality is real. Defying limited security, denying vulnerability, and burying awareness create an unstable vacuum. Flowing into this space is a destructive form of fear, expressing itself through dominating attitudes and behaviors. Our relationships suffer as this *dominating fear* drives us away from the trustful dance of giving, receiving, and giving again.

Early Steps into Dominating Fear

In full flower, the expressions of dominating fear wreak havoc, breeding suspicion and insecurity in all our relationships. Eventually, the gift of limited security gets distorted into something far more threatening: a perception of unlimited insecurity. We then react aggressively when aggression is not appropriate, defensively when not attacked, and strike out preemptively without waiting for an anticipated attack. When fear reaches this stage, the destructiveness is obvious.

This is not the case at the beginning. Earlier in its formation, the roots of dominating fear expressions may not seem harmful at all. The initial key choices we are making are so imperceptible that we would barely notice.

Looking for an easier path to getting what we want, we start drifting into deception. We use flattery or feign interest in another to persuade them to our point of view. We present ourselves in the best possible light by highlighting those personal qualities: competence, compassion, or generosity—that might be valued by the other. At the same time, we minimize or hide those parts of ourselves that spoil the self-portrait we are seeking to project. Before long, this less-than-authentic stance is feeling natural and accurate. Rationalizing and excusing these personal behaviors become easier when we suspect others are engaging us in similar ways.

These early steps on the path of deception are suggesting we can build up our personal security at the expense of those around us. They encourage enhancing our own power for meeting our needs while simultaneously discounting and undermining the interests of others. Slowly, almost imperceptibly, our trustworthiness and our capacity to be trusting are compromised, changing relationships.

This dominating fear-inspired shift also taints our use of labels. We naturally use labels in describing the world around us. Naming and finding labels for the people, places, and things in our world helps us organize our understanding of the world and our place in it. Noting differences in race, sex, age, religion, cultural origin, income, educational level, political views, or other distinguishing markers assists our connecting with and differentiating ourselves from others. When used in this way, the tool of labeling broadens understanding of the diverse gifts of humankind.

Under the influence of dominating fear, we change the function of labeling. Defining others by a label or rigid stereotype turns them into objects; they become tools for building our power or rivals threatening our security.

> Defining others by a label or rigid stereotype turns them into objects; they become tools for building our power or rivals threatening our security.

Framing our relational connections in either of these ways qualitatively changes the character of our interactions. With objectifying labeling, we value other people and our relationships based on what they can do for us or whether they can make contributions to our ongoing security: Can this relationship raise my social appeal? Can it bring me pleasure or boost my self-esteem? Can it offer protection or provide a powerful ally that will help me feel more secure?

Ironically, each of these questions is an implicit acknowledgement of the very human vulnerability and neediness we all share. The distortions of dominating fear move us away from this more honest awareness. Under its influence, we embrace the many manipulations that help us use others for meeting our short-term wants while forgetting we are actually needy ourselves.

This objectifying labeling is problematic from any number of vantage points. Not only promoting a denial of our own vulnerabilities, it inhibits us from recognizing the unique gifts, real contributions, and authentic relationships we could have with the "other." When making assessments of others based on superficial or partial characterizations, we shrink the pool of available relationships, limiting our hospitality to a more exclusive group. This impoverishes our living.

Even more troubling is the way our growing objectification of others sets the stage for more destructive expressions of dominating fear. As we shift from seeing others as persons to seeing them as objects, their personal feelings and perceptions become less important to us. Their sensitivities soon become exploitable tools for enhancing our own security. Once we discount the personhood of others, everything that follows seems all the less troubling and more excusable in our thinking.

The horrific events of the Holocaust followed a nation's objectification of Jews. It is a short step from objectifying labeling to exploitations of the vulnerability in others and the destructive fruits of racism, sexism, religious and cultural persecution, and the many forms of passive-aggressive and outright-aggressive coerciveness. The more we view the other person as an object, the easier it is to justify any means of using them in pursuing our own power and security.

> The more we view the other person as an object, the easier it is to justify any means of using them in pursuing our own power and security.

Not all acts of using others carry the same potential for harm. Some are so common and routine that we might not judge them negatively at all. No one would equate the harmless-seeming, minor manipulations of others with the clearly destructive activities of sexual, economic, or systematic exploitations of the innocent and defenseless. But wherever particular acts of using others might fall on a continuum, they are still fruits of dominating fear. They insert some level of distrust and suspiciousness into every relationship they touch. Labeling and objectifying others do little toward ensuring our long-term security. After all, objectifying other persons is not a one-way street.

When I am viewing someone else as an object, my action draws out their own tendencies to view me as an object. My attempts at using them for my purposes will naturally be reciprocated. These strategies produce a net diminishment of security for everyone involved. All parties in this dance become more vulnerable and insecure—not less.

The logic of this outcome seems continually to escape us. Our ongoing insecurities, along with the urgings of our dominating fear, will keep us on this relationally destructive path. We continue to use others for strengthening and building our personal power, bolstering our sense of security, and avoiding conscious awareness of our own vulnerability.

Tearing Down Others and Exploiting Their Vulnerabilities

Using other people to build up my own security represents only one side of dominating fear. The other side is using my personal power for tearing down and weakening other people, exposing their vulnerability and using the power of domination to coerce them. Getting them to do what I want helps me feel more secure in the moment. With this dimension of dominating fear, I no longer use the other's strengths in building my strength, but instead use their weaknesses against them. If the other person can be weakened or made to appear weaker, then I am improving my own standing and will feel more powerful and secure.

Like the strategy of using the strengths of others in boosting my own power, tearing down others and exploiting their weaknesses may not seem particularly harmful in its early expressions. After all, offering constructive criticism or inviting another to accountability can be a positive way of building them up and calling out their highest potential. Dominating fear sidetracks this life-enhancing purpose into something hurtful and destructive.

The early roots of tearing down others can be seen as we cultivate a critical and fault-finding spirit in relation to others. We start by directing the focus of our attention on what we think is wrong with another person or larger group. We may be asserting that our intentions are constructive, but a closer examination reveals our less-than-pure motives.

Finding fault in others has a double benefit for us—it simultaneously puts the other on the defensive while diverting attention from our own shortcomings. This combination, a frequent tactic in bullying, can elevate our standing in the eyes of bystanders. Framing our role as "the superior helper assisting the inferior one needing our help," can give an additional boost to our own relative power and sense of security.

None of this may be our stated intent. We may be relating in this other-demeaning way with little conscious awareness of the dynamics of the interaction or the hurt it can inflict. These hurtful interactions can emerge in our closest and most important relationships.

> Hurtful interactions can emerge in our closest and most important relationships.

I was personally reminded of this truth and my own weaknesses at the very time I was editing this section. I had criticized the timing of my wife's planned activity, and this had been the last straw for her. She responded, informing me of her recent experience of our interactions. She had experienced me to be short, critical, and demeaning whenever she would relay her own plans or express her ideas. I was surprised and hurt by this disclosure.

Didn't she know I would never intentionally respond in this manner? I became defensive, critical, and demeaning as I denied the truthfulness of her assessment. For hours, I stewed over this affront to my self-perception... too many hours later it dawned on me. Whether or not she had accurately perceived my previous interactions, there could be little doubt that my current reactions to her honest sharing were the same hurtful behaviors she had been describing. I was using these same tearing-down behaviors toward the one I loved. Humbled and shamefaced, I could only apologize for my actions, thank her for her vulnerable honesty, and resolve to be more attuned to my own capacity for expressing fear through domination.

Another expression of dominating fear is intolerance for the limitations and imperfections found in others. This impatience verbally or nonverbally communicates that the other is never quite "good enough" or adequately doing the task. Temporarily, this may provoke the other person into doing more or trying harder, but the longer-term effect is often discouragement, feelings of inadequacy, and a desire for giving up. Resentment, bitterness, and seething anger may boil up in the recipient too.

Communicating our impatience with others' shortcomings may generate a momentary rush of power-filled feelings in us, but this fleeting sensation rarely lasts. What often does last is the resentful anger our actions stimulate in others. When resentfulness is harbored by others or cultivated by our own hurts, it nourishes the seeds that are growing more distrust and more insecurity.

One common expression of this resentful anger is sarcasm. Often subtle and seemingly passive, it can impart a venomous bite while leaving some plausible deniability if its target confronts the speaker. A response of "Oh, I was only joking" allows the sarcastic speaker to separate him or herself from the viciousness of the comment while still inflicting hurt. While a few incidents of sarcasm in a relationship might be excused as unintended hurt or poor usage of humor, an ongoing pattern of sarcastic cuts and putdowns plants new seeds of anger and distrust.

Sarcasm can easily transition into cynicism—a longer lasting and more hurtful "sibling" in this destructive family. Like sarcasm, cynicism is often a product of our own anger bubbling up from genuine hurts or the merely perceived slights we have received from others. Sarcasm, especially in its incidental unpatterned form, seems to have a closer connection to specific events of resentment—it is more time-limited in its expression.

Cynicism, in contrast, draws from a more generalized resentfulness that is no longer tied to specific events. Cynicism turns this generalized resentfulness into a darkened and demeaning lens for evaluating the character and motives of everyone around us. Now more than just an isolated behavior, it colors the way we see and interact with the world.

Cynicism lowers our expectations of the potential good in both others and ourselves while offering itself as a protection from being disappointed or manipulated. Anticipating the worst in others may indeed help us to avoid disappointing surprises, but it also erects and solidifies distrustful barriers that inhibit life-giving relationships. Cynicism also seems to spread like a virus, infecting others with its life-sapping perspective, deflating joy and hope.

If cynicism were merely an attitude, its direct relational destructiveness would be limited to the misery and unhappiness routinely "enjoyed" by its practitioners. Unfortunately, once cynicism becomes the lens for seeing the world around us, it further reshapes our perception of others and ourselves. We can then take "objectification of others" to new levels and can so disorient our moral compass that previously intolerable hurtful actions toward others become acceptable as we anticipate others' hurtfulness toward us. The more cynicism takes hold, the more its stance of suspicion and distrust becomes the primary way of relating to the larger world.

> The more cynicism takes hold, the more its stance of suspicion and distrust becomes the primary way of relating to the larger world.

This worldview of suspicious distrust makes cynicism the launching point for the most destructive expressions of dominating fear. As the distrust and suspicion embodied in cynicism spreads contagiously to a wider audience, it creates its own unsafe and violent world. A suspicious and distrustful eye toward others requires constant vigilance both in identifying potential violence directed toward us and justifying the preemptive violence we may direct toward others. As others caught in this spreading web of cynical suspiciousness embrace a similar worldview, the probability of greater and growing violence expands. There is little incentive for checking its growth or de-escalating the suspiciousness and distrust. Instead, this fear-inspired worldview extends itself in a self-reinforcing pattern where distrust breeds more suspiciousness. All the fruits of relational destructiveness closely follow.

We might prefer discounting this ill-fated picture of the fruits of dominating fear—distrustful suspiciousness and all its repulsive and destructive fallout. But an honest appraisal acknowledges that this process is at work, fueling almost any relational conflict we might observe. The same suspiciousness ignites and perpetuates economic wars and armed conflict on the international stage impacting millions, familial fights touching only individuals, and group conflicts (business, religious, cultural, racial, or political) of any size in between. Whether the violence perpetuated is physically harmful or concentrates its viciousness on tearing down the spirit, the end result remains the same: insecurity spreads in an ever-widening wave, heightening our sense of weakness and vulnerability.

Avoiding awareness of weakness and vulnerability burdens us with a greater sense of vulnerability. How might we respond to this dilemma? Though some suggest that the very definition of insanity is doing the same destructive behavior and expecting a different result, the common response to human vulnerability is staying on the avoidant and destructive path. In continuing on this path, we deploy our imaginations in overriding and getting around the other human limits in resources, knowledge, and choice. We also find new forms of destructive fear.

Questions for Reflection

1. Recall a time when "bad news" was hard for you to accept. What vulnerability might you have been protecting?
2. Describe a situation where your heightened vigilance only increased your sense of vulnerability.
3. How does objectifying labeling inhibit resolution of conflict in politics, in business, in religious communities, or in our own family? How might seeing the personhood of the "adversary" change the dynamics of the interactions?
4. How have tearing-down behaviors impacted your relationships with yourself or with others?

Window from Scripture

The Parable of a Rich Man
(Luke 12:13-21)

This story shines a light on the greed and materialistic mindset evident in every generation. Jesus exposes the fragile hold we have on any of our possessions and their power to possess us and distract us from the true purpose of our living.

> Someone in the crowd said to him, "Teacher, tell my brother to divide the family inheritance with me." But he said to him, "Friend, who set me to be a judge or arbitrator over you?" And he said to them, "Take care! Be on your guard against all kinds of greed; for one's life does not consist in the abundance of possessions." Then he told them a parable: "The land of a rich man produced abundantly. And he thought to himself, 'What should I do, for I have no place to store my crops?' Then he said, 'I will do this: I will pull down my barns and build larger ones, and there I will store all my grain and my goods. And I will say to my soul, Soul, you have ample goods laid up for many years; relax, eat, drink, be merry.' But God said to him, 'You fool! This very night your life is being demanded of you. And the things you have prepared, whose will they be?' So it is with those who store up treasures for themselves but are not rich toward God."

"One's life does not consist in the abundance of possessions." With these words, Jesus brings into question a seemingly unquestionable assumption driving our insatiably possessive and materialistic culture. Does not our culture teach us to look at what we have, and what we can acquire as the truest measure of our worth? Are not many of our lives consumed in the task of holding tightly to what we already have, working to expand what is "ours," and comparing our relative holdings to the holdings of others?

In this parable, we find a man who is fully invested in these cultural assumptions. He possesses an "I" complex (note the many references to himself), and is fully pleased with and focused on himself. Seeing the wealth he apparently possesses, he concludes he is free to build bigger barns, store his surplus grain, and "relax, eat, drink, [and] be merry." The foolishness of his self-absorbed perspective is exposed when pronouncement is made of his unexpected and untimely demise. What he thought he possessed and claimed as his—his life, his stuff, and the time to enjoy them—was actually a set of gifts held in trust.

Having forgotten the Giver and source of all he received, he had pursued personal possession of the gifts rather than joining with the Giver and sharing these gifts with the wider world. Disconnected from the Giver's intended purpose and held tightly in this man's self-absorbed clutches, these once promising gifts became wasted and worthless. His foolish pursuit of possessiveness and the ever-tighter grasping of the gifts had only resulted in the spoiling and corrupting of the possessor—himself—and the gifts he attempted to possess.

Though he might provide an extreme example, the grasping spirit he reflects is familiar to us all. Not only was this spirit evident within the person in the crowd who sought Jesus' help in settling a dispute of inheritance, but it may also be a constant companion in many of our daily interactions. The reach of this spirit is not limited to physical things. Sometimes we may grip most tightly the grudges we hold against others, regrets we carry about the past, or destructive habits and ideas we maintain. What if we reconnected with the Giver's intended purpose, seeing our "possessions" as gifts we loosely hold in trust so we can share and meet the needs of those around us?

Chapter 3
Turning the Gift of Limited Resources into Grasping Fear

Pursuing Possessions

Being human is an amazing gift! Our understanding of that gift profoundly impacts what we do with it. Will we join the dance of giving, receiving, and giving again with trust—seeing our individual humanity as a personalized expression of a gift given for sharing with the world? Or, will we see our individual humanity as our own personal gift that we tightly guard and selfishly use for ourselves? We divert ourselves from the more life-giving path when we make distrustful responses to the vulnerabilities that come with being human.

Expressions of dominating fear objectify, use, or tear down others, providing the most direct responses to those vulnerabilities exposed by limited security. Magnifying our own power and dominating others lets us momentarily forget that we are weak and vulnerable ourselves. *Limited resources* expose a different kind of vulnerability. Our response may be more indirect, pursuing a possessive relationship with material objects, other people, or abstract ideas and entities. The simple act of owning gives us, as the possessor, a perception of being more secure. This possession functions as an outer ring of defense, providing an insulating layer of protection around any perceived vulnerability—whether real or imagined. As a result, our core reason for possession may not be the possessed object itself. Our true motivation may be the more deeply held desire of possessing a greater sense of security.

While we might pursue individual possessions as we build this insulating wall, no particular possession is able to provide a sense of security for very long. Over time, any possession's perceived protective effect diminishes. Like a growing drug tolerance, we require more of a particular possession or more of other possessions to maintain the same effect. The fleeting buzz from claiming something else soon fades and the pursuit of "having more" becomes a never-ending task. We are always chasing a moving target—the more we have, the more we seem to want.

If we were to stop for a moment and consider the futility of this pursuit, we might change our relationship with potential possessions. We might suspend the mindless pursuit entirely or hold what we do possess more loosely. We might exhibit a willingness to share them with others. This radical shift might be wise, but applying it is hard. Once our vulnerability and related insecurities start us down this futile path of pursuing "more," changing course becomes ever more difficult.

> Once our vulnerability and related insecurities start us down the futile path of pursuing "more," changing course becomes ever more difficult.

The targets for our acquisition are not limited to material things. We can claim ownership in people, ideas, and abstract entities. Anyone or anything can be a candidate for our possessiveness if we can intertwine them with our sense of self or they can offer some insulation from feeling vulnerable.

For example, we are probably exercising this kind of possessiveness when perceiving the attitudes or behaviors of our spouses, children, or others to be somehow reflecting upon us. When these in our sphere of influence are responding consistent with our desires, our self-security is built up and enhanced. If, in contrast, their actions are contrary to our desires or expectations, this may prompt a disproportionate anger within us. Our energized reaction can be revealing. Is the intensity of our anger triggered by their act itself, or more by the way their act reflects negatively on some image we hold about ourselves? When it is the latter, our possessive ownership of them is playing a bigger role in our relationship with them than the valuing of their individuality, personhood, and autonomy.

In a similar way to these possessive relationships with people, we can align ourselves with abstract entities. Contenders for this sort of personal "ownership" might include beliefs we hold about philosophical or religious ideas, loyalties we maintain with businesses or educational institutions, or the continuing investments of time and money we make in supporting community organizations or favorite sports teams. Claiming a sense of ownership in one or more of these—feeling like we are a part of something bigger—has a way of quieting our insecurities and reassuring any concerns we may harbor about our own lack of importance. Like undue ownership in relationship to people, the protective energy and disproportionate anger generated when these abstract entities are questioned or challenged is a sure sign that we have taken personal ownership of them. The energy within our reactions is demonstrating that our defensiveness is not just about protecting the individual entity from the challenge: it is protecting a part of us.

Despite its destructive potential, this capacity for claiming ownership or possession is not bad in itself. This is one of the fundamental gifts that make us human. A capacity to claim ownership is necessary if we are joining meaningfully in the dance of giving, receiving, and giving again with trust. I cannot truly give something away unless it first belongs to me. What would be the gift in "giving" something if it actually belonged to someone else? I also cannot truly receive something unless I have the capability of taking ownership of it. This capacity for claiming ownership remains essential in both giving and receiving; the life-giving freedom and trust within the "dance" requires it.

Turning the Gift of Limited Resources into Grasping Fear

> A capacity to claim ownership is necessary if we are joining meaningfully in the dance of giving, receiving, and giving again with trust.

Here is the problem: Similar to other gifts, this capacity to claim ownership can and often does drift from its intended purpose. Self-absorbed possessiveness and never-satisfying acquisitions twist and distort this fundamental human gift into a life-robbing prison of insecurity. Relying on the false but still enticing promise that having more will make us more secure, we exchange this gift's intended gentle grip on possessions for a tighter grasping and guarding possessiveness. This exchange short-circuits the trust-filled dance, leaving us even more insecure as it plants the seeds of further insecurity.

The source of this ever-growing insecurity is the constant presence of three fundamental realities accompanying this bent toward possessiveness and acquiring more. Each alone would undermine security, but as a group they create a self-reinforcing path of insecurity where each lays the groundwork for and perpetuates the others. The first is the obvious—but still easy to forget—reality that pursuing "having more" is a never-ending task. Having more, we want more. Adding to our collection does little to increase our sense of satisfaction or security. It actually makes us more susceptible to the influence of the second reality: limited resources.

If we lived in a world of unlimited resources, additions to our own collection would have little impact on others; their acquisitions would have little impact on us. We would be free in pursuing "having more" without having to consider the needs and interests of those around us. But this is not our world. The pool of resources is limited and this scarcity of resources creates competition for those limited resources. In this competition, my claiming possession of a particular resource is simultaneously thwarting the claim that any other person may have for the same resource. Competition also has a way of shifting and reconfiguring the relative value of resources. My own claim to something often makes that same item seem more valuable and desirable in the eyes of others. The escalation of this competitive rivalry can leave each of us feeling less secure in our own holdings. We clutch what we do possess more tightly and guard it ever more suspiciously.

The third of these realities may very well be the underlying driver of all three realities: the possibility of loss. Much like the terrorizing sense of weakness exposed by limited security, the threat of loss strikes at a primary vulnerability of human existence. Anything and everything we might value or possess is vulnerable to being lost, being taken, or disappearing altogether. No possession, regardless of what it is or how tightly it is held, has the lasting power to insulate, protect, or make us completely secure. Every relationship of possession—whether with people, with abstract entities, or with material things—is subject to change and loss.

Recognizing Gratitude

This possibility of loss can certainly magnify our perception of vulnerability, but it does not necessarily produce the tightly clutching possessiveness that refuses to let go. It also contains seeds that can transform those same insecurities. The same sense of potential loss that sparks concern of "something" being taken from us can also prompt feelings of gratitude that we have been given a time-limited opportunity of receiving and holding that "something" as a gift. How we frame the potential loss is up to us. Seeing our "something" as a gift inspires a genuine gratitude, fundamentally changing the way we understand our relationships with all we "possess."

Unlike insincere expressions of appreciation that may be more about social correctness, this quality of gratitude comes from the depths of the heart and becomes both a way of seeing and a focused choice. Gratitude recognizes that what we have is an unmerited gift of grace we hold in trust. The common approach to possessions is seeing them as the well-deserved and directly earned fruit of our labors—gratitude looks deeper and pictures a larger reality. It recognizes the underlying, unmerited grace giving us the ability to exercise that hard work.

> Gratitude recognizes that what we have is an unmerited gift of grace we hold in trust.

What if we were to see ourselves as graced stewards of all we have received rather than entitled earners? What if we were willing to live with an attitude of trusting that future needs would be supplied as needed? If we could live in this graced perspective, we would no longer have to hold tightly to our possessions or drive ourselves constantly to acquire more.

Furthering its benefit, this transforming gratitude would disarm threats that actualized losses and even potential losses can bring to our sense of identity and personal worth. With gratitude, we would no longer need to value and define ourselves based upon the breadth of our possessions because this chosen spirit would allow us to find value through the relationship of trust we have with the Giver. When our true sense of worth comes through this gratitude-infused relationship, we are not threatened or diminished by the losses we experience.

This does not mean that any grief associated with loss is eliminated. We still grieve, but gratitude changes the way we grieve. Grief, as it is commonly observed, resentfully rails against all the consequences and perceived injustices brought about by a change or loss. At the same time, it may still hold these resentments tightly, refusing to let them go. As a chaplain, I have seen many people whose grief in a new loss was complicated and intensified by past losses they would not release. This pattern only magnifies and extends their pain.

A friend tells a story that offers a contrast. George (not his real name), his sixteen-year-old relative, had died of a broken neck in a freak accident while playfully wrestling with a best friend. The best friend, George's family, and the whole community were devastated by the loss. George's father spoke at the funeral. While recognizing the terrible loss and death's ending of his future hopes and dreams for his son, he also spoke words of gratitude: "I am grateful to God for giving us our son for the sixteen years he was with us." A gratitude-infused grief like this acknowledges loss with thankfulness for all the gifts brought by that former "possession" held for a time as a trust. Gratitude-infused grief helps us let go, not forgetting but allowing us to fill the empty space with new gifts that come into our possession. These new gifts can be received with a renewing gratitude and loosely held, hopeful trust.

The benefits of choosing this quality of genuine gratitude are inviting, but they do not come without cost. This spirit of thankfulness is rooted in the awareness of our complete dependence upon the Giver and the limits given to humanity. We cannot choose gratitude without coming to terms with our human limitations and vulnerabilities. Choosing gratitude requires trust and humility, acknowledging we are indeed vulnerable, needy, and insecure in our own strength. A transforming gratitude is inextricably wedded to the constant awareness of our human vulnerability.

While costs associated with genuine gratitude may be significant, the lack of it carries even heavier costs. Without gratitude, we stay on the treadmill of seeking more, continuing the competitive battles with others for scarce resources. Worst of all, we convert the possibility of loss into a constant and open-ended threat where every potential loss becomes threatening. Without gratitude to help us disconnect our sense of personhood from what we "possess," every loss—whether real or merely anticipated—threatens to diminish our security and worth, while leaving us ever more vulnerable and exposed.

> Without gratitude to help us disconnect our sense of personhood from what we "possess," every loss—whether real or merely anticipated—threatens to diminish our security and worth, while leaving us ever more vulnerable and exposed.

This process creates a threat of loss that becomes an ongoing, all-encompassing threat for which there is no defense. If we add up all these costs, we can make a great case for choosing gratitude and its commonsense solution addressing limited resources and the related insecurities that plague us.

But a challenge remains. Although human vulnerability, neediness, and insecurity may seem obvious to an objective observer, this truth is still not easy to accept. Much as we might avoid conscious awareness of vulnerability to harm, we are also tempted to resist awareness of a complete threat of loss. Both sources of vulnerability highlight the limitedness of our human power in protecting our physical selves or the things we value. Giving attention to the threat of loss only seems to add to an already discomforting sense of insecurity. The enticing solution is avoiding conscious awareness of its presence, allowing it to mold and shape our choices and behaviors in unconscious ways.

Regrettably, giving in to this temptation and pushing the threat of loss below the surface has its own set of far-reaching consequences. Just as avoiding awareness of the threat of harm associated with limited security fosters development of dominating fear expressions, so avoiding the vulnerability uncovered by the threat of loss cultivates expressions of *grasping fear*. With this latter form of fear we grasp, we guard, and we react in logic-defying ways. Undermining and harming relationships of every kind, both expressions of fear inflict their greatest harm when destroying the foundation of trust underlying our closest relationships.

Grasping Expressions of Fear

Akin to expressions of dominating fear, the expressions of grasping fear may not reveal their most destructive elements until long after they have been introduced. Though carrying the roots of all they can potentially become from the beginning, it is their cumulative effect that makes them so destructive. Dominating expressions of fear generally assert their power and move on to the next challenge. Grasping expressions never seem able to let go and prompt an ever-tightening grip on our possessions until our possessions come to possess us.

The fear conveyed through grasping, as with other expressions of destructive fear, finds its roots in avoiding awareness of human vulnerability and limitation. Its primary strategies—grasping, holding, and guarding—present themselves as a short-term fix for managing insecurity. Just as a small child may hold on to a favorite toy or blanket and find reassurance in the comfort of that object, so we, over time, come to associate reassurance and comfort with holding objects in our possession. If one object enhances our sense of security, then surely two will provide even more. Conversely, if we lose one of what we already have, then our sense of security seems diminished by the loss. Before long, these associations influence our behaviors and the reinforcing pattern of grasping and holding begins perpetuating itself.

Initially in the formation of this pattern, grasping—acquiring more—appears to have the greater influence. The threat of loss seems to have less sway when our pile of acquisitions is small. Is it not easier taking risks when we have nothing to lose? But as our acquisitions grow, the balance shifts—the threat of loss grows in influence and power. Eventually, the threat of loss becomes the greater driving force. Once this happens, we will expend far more energy to keep from losing something we have than to add one more thing to our acquisitions. This seems to have been the issue for the "ruler" who came to Jesus seeking "eternal life" (see Luke 18:18-23). When Jesus told him he lacked one thing and to "sell all that you own and distribute the money to the poor," the man "became sad; for he was very rich."

The growing power of the threat of loss also prompts a shift in our relationships with what we possess. Initially, our possessions serve as *a* source of security, enriching our living and providing a level of comfort and reassurance. As the threat of loss gains traction, these possessions may become *the* source of our security. No longer mere objects seeming to enhance our worth, they become the measures of our worth and the scales we use for measuring our value. As this plays out, we start believing that the more we have and can hold in our grasp, the more valuable we are. The opposite may become equally powerful in our perception. If these become our scales for self-assessment, our having less or losing more shrinks our perceived sense of value and worth.

> We start believing that the more we have and can hold in our grasp, the more valuable we are.

Initially, this shift in self-valuing might seem subtle and insignificant. Once what we hold becomes the source of our security, our relationship with these possessions qualitatively changes. If we are allowing these possessions to be measures of our worth, we are also inviting them to have godlike power over our lives. Giving them functioning authority over our lives does not require a literal bowing down and worshiping of our possessions. But anytime we base our self-definition on what we have or what we lack, we are turning away from the Giver and pledging allegiance to this god of our possessions. The more we tie our self-value to what we possess, the more tightly we hold on to our possessions and the more difficulty we will have in letting go.

Much of the time this would not be a conscious process. We might even deny that our pool of possessions exercises this kind of power in our lives. As with other expressions of destructive fear, these grasping fear responses eventually become so intertwined with our lives that we may be unable to see the power of their influence. What can be seen is the tenacious grip we maintain on what we possess and the seeming inability or unwillingness to release them.

The most obvious evidence of this unrelenting grip is the relationships we develop with concrete, material objects. Homes, vehicles, technology, and other material things are observable with our senses and easily quantified and converted into monetary values. They soon become prime and enticing targets for our acquisitive tastes. These outward expressions of value come to represent the measure of our perceived worth (or lack of worth) to the world at large.

Adopting this standard of worth quickly turns it into a tool of comparison. Once this self-measure is activated, it not only urges us to acquire more, but it also urges us to acquire more than those around us. This comparative standard of worth promotes an endless list of behaviors that fall on a continuum from the seemingly harmless to the blatantly injurious and illegal. We might debate about where these particular instances would be on the continuum, but money-based workaholism, distorting and manipulating for monetary gain, white-collar fraud, and violent robbery would all find their roots in its urgings.

Once we "have more," we create new challenges. We must protect and secure what we have. If we are following this standard, any loss for us represents a gain for someone else and a diminishment of our own worth. Having more forces us to tighten our grip another notch tighter.

But this brings an ironic twist. Securing our holdings more tightly prompts us to lose our grip on who we truly are and the consequences of our actions. We miss the bigger picture, narrowing our focus as we try to satisfy the relentless and insatiable taskmaster—grasping fear—urging us to pursue any and every means to guard our possessions from any potential rival. The spirit of suspiciousness this generates will sow distrust into every relationship it touches.

> Securing our holdings more tightly prompts us to lose our grip on who we truly are and the consequences of our actions.

The reach of this taskmaster on our relationships with material objects may vary with each individual, but it is hard for any of us to escape completely from its influence. The loss of perspective it generates distorts our vision of both others and ourselves. We may easily identify this destructive fruit in others, but we have trouble seeing it in ourselves.

Grasping fear is most observable with concrete, material possessions but these may not exhibit the most harmful aspects of its influence. We can also apply this spirit in our relationships with other people. Any time I treat others as if they exist to meet my needs, I am taking on a functional ownership role in relation to them. We can observe this in parenting relationships with children, spouses with one another, or employers with their employees.

In milder forms of this possessiveness, exercising undue control, exhibitions of jealousy, or displays of suspicion might be framed as "overprotectiveness" or even expressions of love and concern. Any actual harm here might easily be discounted or excused. As we move down the continuum and these behaviors grow in intensity, their destructiveness becomes undeniable. In their most malignant forms, we see the horrible damage unleashed in the physical, emotional, and sexual abuse of domestic violence. Here, both grasping and dominating expressions of fear collaborate, producing a destructiveness impacting everyone involved for generations.

> With domestic violence, both grasping and dominating expressions of fear collaborate, producing a destructiveness impacting everyone involved for generations.

While the harm in these latter cases is obvious, it would be misleading to conclude that milder displays of grasping behavior are harmless. At every level on the continuum, fear behaviors directed at others are attempting to mold them in certain directions, treating them as objects rather than valuing their personhood and autonomy. Grasping fear behaviors undermine the trust required for building and maintaining lasting, life-giving relationships. Our efforts of holding others tightly also let go of the very component—trust—inviting and enabling them to remain close to us by their own choice. A tight and coercive grip would never be needed where trust remains abundant.

> A tight and coercive grip would never be needed where trust remains abundant.

Expressions of grasping fear also turn self-destructive with the harboring of bitterness and unforgiveness against others. Here, we tightly hold a self-absorbed and self-righteous appraisal of events, refusing to release others from actions we perceive have been hurtful to us. We may hold grudges against others for intentional injuries, unintended harms, and hurts perceived only by us and completely unknown to them.

Harboring these hurts and holding them tighter—even when the hurts may be legitimate—only serve to keep old wounds open, inflicting new wounds upon ourselves or the innocent people who happen to be around us at the time. In the end, the bitterness and unforgiveness we hold may have little impact on our intended targets; they may not even know what we are holding or why we keep holding it. Harboring bitterness and unforgiveness only hurts and destroys us. Like a caustic acid or poison, it eats away and kills the life of the one who holds it.

Sometimes, this spirit of bitterness and unforgiveness is turned inward toward ourselves. We focus on our flaws or particular aspects of our own story that we cannot or will not release. We keep replaying past mistakes, missed opportunities, or painful interactions with other people even as we cling to the false hope that we might somehow rewrite or change what has already happened. Not only is this endless replaying a fruitless endeavor in itself, but holding tightly to an often-self-defacing understanding of events also inhibits consideration of more life-giving interpretations. We can cling so tightly to our life-limiting perceptions of our past that we have little energy left for facing the challenges and opportunities of the present and future.

The ever-tightening grip inspired by expressions of grasping fear distorts our relationships with material things, other people, and our own selves. Our possessions can come to possess us. We might have pursued possessing to insulate ourselves from the insecurities of human limitation, but this ever-tightening grip only lays the groundwork for further insecurity and additional expressions of fear.

Questions for Reflection

1. How has your own pursuit of "having more" impacted your relationships and your spiritual well-being?
2. How has gratitude assisted in your coping with life losses? How has gratitude loosened the hold that "possessions" might have held on your life?
3. When has the pursuit of a material good or life goal sidetracked you or someone you have known from more important values?
4. How has holding on to bitterness or unforgiveness impacted relationships in your life or in the life of someone you have known?

A Window from Scripture

The Hazards of Public "Righteousness"
(Matt. 6:1-8, 16-18)

The lure of image management can be enticing. In this excerpt from the Sermon on the Mount, Jesus invites his hearers and each of us to examine the real motives for our actions. It is tempting to substitute what we would like to be true for what actually is true.

> (Jesus said) "Beware of practicing your piety before others in order to be seen by them; for then you have no reward from your Father in heaven.
> "So whenever you give alms, do not sound a trumpet before you, as the hypocrites do in the synagogues and in the streets, so that they may

be praised by others. Truly I tell you, they have received their reward. But when you give alms, do not let your left hand know what your right hand is doing, so that your alms may be done in secret; and your Father who sees in secret will reward you.

"And whenever you pray, do not be like the hypocrites; for they love to stand and pray in the synagogues and at the street corners, so that they may be seen by others. Truly I tell you, they have received their reward. But whenever you pray, go into your room and shut the door and pray to your Father who is in secret; and your Father who sees in secret will reward you.

"When you are praying, do not heap up empty phrases as the Gentiles do; for they think that they will be heard because of their many words. Do not be like them, for your Father knows what you need before you ask him.

"And whenever you fast, do not look dismal, like the hypocrites, for they disfigure their faces so as to show others that they are fasting. Truly I tell you, they have received their reward. But when you fast, put oil on your head and wash your face, so that your fasting may be seen not by others but by your Father who is in secret; and your Father who sees in secret will reward you."

With his directive to "Beware of practicing your piety before others in order to be seen by them," Jesus demonstrates great insight into human nature. He recognizes that we are most vulnerable to self-deception and the exercising of our capacity to deceive others when we are assessing our own acts that might appear good and holy. Providing three examples—giving to the needy, praying, and fasting—Jesus reminds us that careful, honest attentiveness to our true motives is required if we are to actualize the fullest benefit of these acts of goodness. If not, we are in constant danger of having even these good works devolve into fruitless tasks of meaningless hypocrisy.

Appearances can be and often are deceiving. Imagining our own selves in a more positive light or projecting a more affirming image to others can be enticing. It is far easier to appear to be good or holy than to actually be good or holy. With the help of our imaginations, we are able to fool others and ourselves into believing what we portray ourselves to be. In our imaginations, our motives can always be pure, our actions can always be right, and our vulnerabilities can always be hidden. Imagination is not constrained by the limitations that truth brings.

Jesus offers a reversal of this common pattern of image management. Rather than projecting an illusion of ourselves that hides from truth, misleading and fooling both others and ourselves, Jesus invites us to reveal our true self to the Unseen One. This One cannot be fooled, knows us with all our flaws, and still views each of us with transforming love and grace. Were we to accept this invitation of grace, would we not be freed from the tyranny of managing appearance and a need to hide our true self from our own selves and the world around us?

Jesus' invitation, while always available, may not be so easily embraced; we may still choose to reject it. Why maintain the many burdens of "keeping up appearances" and all the self-deceptions and misrepresentations that these require of us? Why keep hiding truth from our own selves and others? Does this pattern of deception give us what we truly need?

Chapter 4
Turning the Gift of Limited Knowledge into Lying Fear

The Dance of Imagination and Knowledge

Being human is an amazing gift! Within this larger gift are many other gifts. It is a gift to be able to see and recognize the giftedness of being human, to see and evaluate our own selves, and to see and retain this knowledge. These "seeing" abilities employ the supportive gifts of perception, interpretation, and judgment; the gift of imagination enhances each one. Working together, all of these expressions of gift are essential for the dance of giving, receiving, and giving again with trust.

The "seeing" we are describing does not depend on physical eyes. Each relies instead on the abstract eye of the mind for "seeing" realities that only have substance in our minds. These "seeing" gifts bring choices: Will we live within the limits of our current knowledge base and the constraints of actual truth, or will we avoid the vulnerabilities truth exposes—manipulating, distorting, and hiding truth about ourselves from both others and ourselves? The avoidant choice entices in the moment, but ultimately disturbs the dance of trust, sowing seeds of distrust and distorting our ability to see accurately with our mind's eye.

Physical sight is easier to understand and describe. Being a gift for humans and non-humans alike, physical sight gives one the ability to interact with the material world. For some non-human creatures, this ability permits seeing depth and detail far exceeding the physical sight available to human beings. For these, survival depends upon seeing in minimal light or detecting slight movements of food sources or predators. But physical sight remains limited: it only permits the seeing of concrete and tangible objects in the physical world.

Seeing with the mind's eye is a gift allowing us to see far more. While some animals—i.e., our pets—might exhibit simpler forms of this gift, its more complex form is unique to humans. Imagination allows us to see and grasp ideas, consider and formulate interpretations, and determine and make judgments.

As we might imagine (pun intended), this gift of imagination provides a powerful tool, expanding our understanding of our own selves and our place in both the physical world and the world of ideas. Unlike animals, having only the warnings and reactivity of instinctual fear protecting them from danger, imagination gives humans the capacity for combining experience, knowledge, and images in our minds. With this expanded capacity, we humans create a more rational and informed fear, permitting us to envision potential dangers and employ possible countering strategies for keeping ourselves safe.

With imagination, we are not bound by the limits of time. We can look backward and change our understanding of an old experience or look forward and try out varying future possibilities in the freedom and creativity of fantasy. Imagination helps us step outside ourselves, expanding our understanding of the many limits constraining us even as it opens up a wider world for us all.

This gift of imagination enhances our living but cannot do its work without assistance. Imagination always has a dance partner: knowledge. This knowledge may come from book learning, observation of the world around us, or personal experience, but all these sources fuel imagination. The interplay between these initial sources and imagination builds a growing knowledge base, spurring further imaginative expansions. In this ongoing creative dance, imagination and knowledge nurture and enhance each other; together, these partners further expand our world of understanding, enabling us to see our world with deeper insight in much the same way that having two eyes gives us the depth perception for seeing our world in three dimensions.

> Imagination always has a dance partner: knowledge.

We can see the interplay of knowledge and imagination when we look at how we learn to read. Before we can start reading, we must first acquire a small vocabulary of words. We learn these words by hearing them, mimicking their sounds and usage, and employing them for communicating our wants and needs. Next, we plant images in our minds that we associate with the words we use. For example, we hear and learn to speak the word "cow" and develop a picture in our mind of what a cow looks like. We connect particular arrangements of letters on a page (ex., "c-o-w") with those images, and these now written words come to represent the objects themselves in our minds, enabling us to read.

This is only the beginning. Once we learn that words on a page can communicate meaning and information, we build an ever-growing vocabulary of written words. The potential collaboration of knowledge and imagination then expands exponentially. Combining knowledge and imagination, we "sound out" and guess the meaning of new written words by seeing how they relate to words we already know. As we discover the patterns of wonderful, boundless combinations of words, we are free to compose and write our own creations of words and sentences, conveying new meanings to others and for ourselves. Using this collaborative process, we move from a world constrained by physical realities to a seemingly unlimited world of ideas and possibility. In similar and innumerable ways, this fruitful dance of imagination and knowledge touches and enriches every aspect of our lives.

Challenges Within This Collaborating Dance

This partnership of imagination and knowledge brings new challenges. First, it sets up an ongoing comparison between our current experienced reality and the better reality we can envision in our imaginations. This comparison could help us make changes that align current reality more in line with the vision. But it can also burden us with unrealistic expectations we might never meet. When these expectations foster a broader sense of dissatisfaction with the here-and-now, they breed their own brand of chronic unhappiness. The perfection of imagined ideals never fits comfortably into the tighter constraints of the actual world; trying to make them fit only frustrates and disappoints.

A second challenge comes through the ever-present limits on acquiring knowledge. The pace of knowledge expansion always trails the speed our imaginations can envision. Our memory capacity and the time required for learning further slows any growth in our personal knowledge. Imagination is not so limited. It has only one limitation: our own willingness to visualize creatively.

> Imagination has only one limitation: our willingness to visualize creatively.

This gap between what we can imagine knowing and what we actually know might motivate us to learn more, but can also highlight the deficiencies in our current knowledge. This can create a problem. If I believe my knowledge base is the measure of my competence and self-worth, I will be threatened when my imagination spotlights any knowledge deficits I might have.

The resulting insecurity prompts new efforts toward either suppressing awareness of these deficits or resisting my imagination's focus on them. Neither of these strategies will succeed. Imagination always stays at least one step ahead. Despite the huge explosion of knowledge available through the Internet and all the advances in computer speed, memory, and search, our store of knowledge can never make up the difference. Knowing more and knowing it faster may help, but our imagination merely adjusts to the new reality, raising the target of expectation.

Both of these challenges remind us that the collaborating dance of knowledge and imagination is a double-edged sword. The same giftedness helping us see and create new possibilities also reveals previously unseen potential vulnerabilities. Our pets, with their more limited imaginative capacity, are spared the concerns we might have about our lodging or next meal, the opinion others might have of us, or our aging process and mortality. A hypersensitive collaborating of imagination and knowledge can lead us into perceiving danger around any corner, whether real or not. It can prompt the suspicious eyeing of the motives and actions of others even when no ill will is actually directed at us. The scope of our worry is only limited by our willingness to imagine.

This increased awareness of vulnerability both discomforts and threatens, disrupting the collaboration of imagination and knowledge gathering. As suspiciousness between the two partners grows, we deny ourselves valuable feedback about our own selves and our place in the world. If they stop working together, we lose the insight and depth perception they could provide.

Even when these two are working together, we still need to exercise discernment as we are assessing what our imagination is telling us. Imagination can move beyond the constraints of truth. In its capacity of imagining a world where limits do not exist, it is free to use "facts" it only imagines to be true for its imaginative expansions. These imaginary "facts" may provide useful and possibility-expanding information as long as they are recognized as imaginative speculations. They take on a different character if they are incorporated into our bank of knowledge as if they are actually accurate fact. Once we allow things we can imagine and would like to be true to be considered "true," our collaboration of knowledge and imagination is creating an alternative reality.

We might observe an example of this in the initial stages of what we affectionately refer to as "falling in love." With an energizing passion, we see the other through "rose-colored glasses," projecting an idealized image of our beloved that could never hold up to the rigors of reality. In imaginative transitions such as this, regular limits can be adjusted and stretched, tempting us then to view this alternate reality as the real thing. But shifting reality this way carries a cost. While the self-deception of "falling in love" may turn out okay, other treks down this self-deceiving path may not. Each time we participate in a changing of "reality," we are also preparing the soil, planting the seed and making possible the destructive fruit of lies that often follows.

Leaving the constraints of truth can be particularly attractive when we perceive we have vulnerabilities at risk of being exposed. Whether these vulnerabilities involve personal security, the safety of our things, or information about ourselves we would rather not have the world know, we may find it easier pretending we are not vulnerable in these areas than living with the uncertainties that come with recognizing their truth. Why live with the discomforts of having weaknesses exposed when I can convince others and myself that I am not so vulnerable?

When the insecurities exposed by an awareness of vulnerability intersect with an enticing escape route offered by an alternative rendering of "truth," this can be just too tempting to pass up. We might enter this descending path into manipulations of truth with seemingly the purest of motives, but continuing on this path rarely keeps our virtue intact. If and when we start yielding to this temptation, this deceptive stance of lying to ourselves and to others is conceived, born, and starts growing a new life of its own in us.

> We might enter the descending path into manipulations of truth with seemingly the purest of motives, but continuing on this path rarely keeps our virtue intact.

This pathway may seem attractive and offer short-term benefits, but the descent into manipulations of truth and the lies that follow is not the only way through the discomforts that awareness of vulnerability evokes. There is a narrow path—a path of acceptance—allowing us to navigate through the challenges coming with the collaboration of imagination and knowledge while still maintaining the fruitful partnership between them.

When we are on this path of trusting acceptance, we are willing to live with reality as it is, relying on an underlying sense of security about our own selves, our place in the world, and the trustworthiness of the Giver. The gaps between current experienced reality and the better reality we can imagine, between what we know and can imagine knowing, and between what is actually true and what we might pretend could be true are not viewed as problems to overcome. Instead, these gaps are seen as potential opportunities allowing us to learn and grow in new directions. When we walk on this trusting path of acceptance, any potentially exposed vulnerability can be seen as a gift that might lead us into deeper understanding. We can celebrate the "not yet known" with the same joy a child might experience when eagerly anticipating the unwrapping of a gift. We can also carry the trusting hope that time and effort can turn the "not yet known" into new knowledge. Maintaining the ongoing trust between these two collaborating partners—imagination and knowledge—this path makes possible and perpetuates the wider joy and hope available through their fruitful and collaborative dance.

This alternative path has its own challenges. Staying on the path of acceptance requires an intentional trusting choice and a willingness to live with the discomforting components of vulnerability. Describing this path may be far easier than practicing the trust it requires. We do live in a world that is often unsafe and untrustworthy in both appearance and reality. The obstacles we encounter on this narrow path will keep urging us to turn it into either a path briefly tried but then abandoned or a path never to be embarked upon at all.

Unlike the steps on the trusting path of acceptance, beginning the descent down the path into manipulations of truth does not require a conscious choice. We drift onto this path of deception when a departure from truth seems easier and less threatening than living with the vulnerabilities that truth might expose. Our original motivation for starting down this path into lying may be more a reflection of our discomfort with vulnerabilities or potential exposures of truth—not a conscious and intentional choice to deceive. Unfortunately, our lack of harmful intent will not shield us from the naturally occurring consequences.

Whether innocent or not, an initial lie requires additional lies to sustain it, and these require further lies to sustain them. This escalating regression continues until it becomes hard for us to distinguish between the actually true and the lies we have created in our imagination. This deceiving process not only undermines our trust in our own knowledge base but also places any previously earned trust from others at risk from a damaging exposure of our lies.

All our efforts toward avoiding exposures of truth propel us toward destructive consequences. As we found in earlier chapters, attempts made to avoid awareness of our vulnerabilities or get around the limits of our humanity also insert the various expressions of destructive fear into our lives and relationships. In a similar way, we cultivate hiding and lying expressions of fear when reacting to limits in our knowledge or threats around exposure of truth.

Hiding with Lying Fear

Each flavor of destructive fear misuses the gift of imagination, departing from truth. This distortion of truth may be playing a more secondary role in expressions of dominating fear and grasping fear, but becomes the primary weapon of choice when our insecurities are urging us to present false images or hide truth from the world. In the beginning, we direct these lies toward others; in the end, we become the deceived ones, being trapped in the hurt of the relational consequences that follow.

As with dominating and grasping expressions of fear, lying fear expressions do not reveal their most destructive forms when first introduced. They start with seemingly harmless alterations in our understanding of genuine reality that might be easy to overlook and excuse. As tiny deviations from truth grow into larger ones, the web of deception becomes more complex and intertwined. Before long, our sensitivity has been dulled and we lose sight of the real truth and the many destructive possibilities.

While we might employ an unlimited variety of hiding and lying strategies associated with this flavor of fear, all of them find root in our discomfort with human vulnerability. One form of hiding is displayed in individuals who are reluctant to use phrases such as "I do not know" or "I was wrong" in personal interactions. This can be a way of hiding from discomforts with admitting limitations in their knowledge base or acknowledging mistakes they have made.

We can see another form of hiding in the often cited gender stereotypes of men who avoid asking directions or women who are obsessed with physical appearance; both stereotypes may actually be describing people who are guarding against exposures of their self-perceived vulnerabilities. Other gender-based stereotypes dictate that "appropriate women" "should" suppress their anger and "big boys don't cry." We are seeing the power of these stereotypes when we observe women who hide their angry feelings by expressing them with tears and "sadness," or conversely, men expressing their sad feelings using "anger."

Turning the Gift of Limited Knowledge into Lying Fear

These particular forms of hiding are clearly stereotypes—and certainly do not apply to all individuals—but they point to perhaps the most common and all-encompassing hiding strategy: disconnecting from our feelings. Fearful, angry, or sad feelings may be suppressed if we have learned to identify these feelings as "negative" and associate them with unwanted events, destructive relational interactions, or other hurtful and discomforting outcomes. Shame and guilt might be avoided for similar reasons.

> Fearful, angry, or sad feelings may be suppressed if we have learned to identify these feelings as "negative" and associate them with unwanted events, destructive relational interactions, or other hurtful and discomforting outcomes.

As a chaplain, I seek to provide a safe space where these feelings can be experienced and named, and can fulfill a healing purpose. I have learned that changing these lifelong disconnecting patterns is not easy. Courage and intentionally are required if we are to face them in healing ways.

Unfortunately, this disconnection from feelings is not limited to these "negative" emotions. The "positive" feelings of heartfelt love, gratitude, or joy might also be suppressed or avoided. This could happen if these life-giving feelings have previously been met with ridicule from significant others or we have received shaming messages that would imply we are somehow not worthy or "good enough" to feel and enjoy them.

Disconnecting and hiding from our feelings might offer a short-term avoidance of discomfort; in the long run, this strategy promotes the creation of even more entrenched forms of dis-ease and brokenness. It robs us of all the gifts these feelings could provide for enriching our relationships with others and deepening our understanding of ourselves. In contrast, the previously described—but rarely chosen—narrow path of trusting acceptance offers a gifting perspective on our emotions. By accepting discomforting realities, this path is recognizing the greater truth that all our feelings—when used and understood appropriately—are purposed toward healing and wholeness.

Appropriate (reality-based) fear is a gift that helps us identify threats; likewise, the gift of appropriate anger energizes us to respond in ways that promote safeness. The gift of sadness, while unpleasant, deepens our understanding of the former gift or change we are grieving, helps us let go of it, and allows a fuller embracing of the new gifts we might receive in the future.

Even guilt and shame, which prompt us to feel bad about what we have done or who we are, provide gifts we need for authentic relationships. Appropriate guilt informs us about a gap between our internal values and our external behaviors—it energizes adjusting one or the other (or both) so that we live with genuineness and integrity. Appropriate shame alerts us when our self-image is based on a lie and we have moved outside the boundaries of our humanness. Shame tells us that either our pride has deceived us into thinking we are more than human (we have effectively claimed personal godhood) or our laziness has misled us into thinking we are less than human. In this latter case, we are failing to hold ourselves accountable for our behavior or our growth.

Seeing the purpose behind appropriate use of our "negative" feelings helps us see the transformative power of exploring and expressing all our feelings in our living. This life-giving understanding opens up new connective possibilities in all our relationships, creating the grounding of trust required for the fullest flowering of our "positive" feelings—love, gratitude, and joy. Unlike the disconnection from feelings and relational deficits produced while hiding, the trust exhibited within this vision gives love and gratitude fuller expression in our relational connections. Love would express our capacity to give ourselves freely, and gratitude our capacity to receive freely from others. When all our gifting emotions are serving and fulfilling their purpose, the genuine and celebratory feelings of joy and gladness can be unleashed.

> When all our gifting emotions are serving and fulfilling their purpose, the genuine and celebratory feelings of joy and gladness can be unleashed.

Like the narrow path of trustful acceptance supporting it, this vision of our feelings working in harmony to deepen our relational connections and self-understanding may be rarely realized in our day-to-day living. Despite the ever-present option of living with and learning from the gifts that our discomforting emotions might surface, it seems easier in the moment to hide from these feelings and avoid the growth and change they might ask of us. After all, hiding does not require conscious thought or intention. We can just passively drift into this hiding stance and detach ourselves from our feelings, cutting off the valuable resource they offer for connecting with and understanding our world.

Much of the hiding we do is not a conscious and intentional choice; it is an almost instinctual reaction to avoid the discomforts coming with vulnerability and knowledge. Slipping into denial, we overlook pertinent facts and piece together dubious bits of information to create and justify an incomplete worldview, helping us to avoid facing discomforting realities. We can observe this in the political arena where each side focuses on the other's blind spots and failures while simultaneously discounting and evading the discomforts exposed by its own. In this denial-filled process, both sides effectively avoid taking responsibility for solving real problems. They each blame the other, and together miss available opportunities for finding collaborative solutions. On a more personal level, we can close our eyes to the very real limitations of our own humanity, maintaining the illusion that we are self-sufficient and denying the power these limitations have over us.

All of these hiding strategies contain elements of deception, but they are primarily deceptions of self. In these reactive efforts to avoid discomfort, we are mostly cheating ourselves as we deprive ourselves of the helpful knowledge that could have been readily available to us. Having hidden from ourselves, we never know what we might have missed.

The discomfort of exposed vulnerability can also prompt a movement beyond a reactive hiding to a more intentional deceptiveness. The feelings of guilt and shame are particularly susceptible to this manipulation. Although guilt and shame can potentially promote growth and healing, these feelings can also seem more personal and thereby more threatening than the other emotions. While fearful, angry, or sad feelings also give us feedback about our experience of the world, guilt and shame may be experienced more as revelations about us personally. They focus on what we have done and pass judgment on what those actions say about who we are.

When influenced by destructive fear, our guilt and shame can alter and distort our perception of other feelings. Fear-tainted guilt and shame can convert any feeling into a personalized reflection of how we see ourselves to be. "I am angry about . . ." is translated into "I am an angry person," or "I did something bad" is turned into "I am bad." The sense of personal vulnerability exposed by this kind of guilt and shame gives us even stronger incentive to avoid this discomfort, urging a more direct strategy: intentional and deceptive lying.

Lying can take many forms. One form is withholding truthful information. We can intentionally keep secrets about what we have done or failed to do and the mistakes we have made. We may fail to disclose our true feelings or let others make false assumptions about our beliefs, our needs, or our hopes for the future. This conscious withholding of information manipulates others and allows us to present ourselves as we would like to be seen so we can get what we want or protect what we have. Even though withholding truthful information may not be lying in a technical sense, it is still knowingly deceptive and undermines trust. It also exposes the withholder to the ever-present risk of having the full truth come out.

A step beyond withholding truthful information is manipulating truthful information in ways that paint us in a better light and shift blame for unwanted aspects onto others. Truth can be distorted when it is revealed selectively or the context is twisted. Numerous examples could again be cited in the political domain on every level. Are there not valid reasons why courts have witnesses sworn to tell "the truth, the whole truth, and nothing but the truth"? Distorting truth may be one step further down the path of deceiving, but it may still be easy to convince ourselves of the general truthfulness of our presentations, overlooking and excusing what are actually deceptive behaviors. After all, what we are saying does appear to be true—from a certain point of view (our own).

The further we travel down this path of deception, the easier it becomes to escalate our deception from "technical" truth telling to outright lying. As noted earlier, imagination is not limited by the constraints of truth. It has the capacity to use "facts" it only imagines being true for creating a more appealing alternative reality. Why be truthful when a lie can get us what we want quicker, easier, and with less apparent discomfort?

> Why be truthful when a lie can get us what we want quicker, easier, and with less apparent discomfort?

As destructive fear urges us, this calculation can seem more and more reasonable, freeing us to create misleading story lines and changing whatever "facts" we need to execute our deceptions. Once actual truth becomes "flexible" in our minds, the scope of lies can expand exponentially. Anything and everything can be used and misused in an ever-expanding web of deception. Once we cut our ties from the anchor of truth, we are free to drift with the currents flowing from an unlimited capacity to lie.

The freedom on this deceptive path offers obvious short-term benefit, but a host of constraining factors complicate the equation. First of all, effective lying requires mixing in a certain amount of actual truth to give credibility to the lies. As time passes, the distinctions between actual truth and the lies we have created may become increasingly blurred in our minds. We may forget what the real truth is, losing track of the lies we have told and those who have heard them.

Managing information becomes even more complicated when those we have lied to start communicating with each other—we need more and more lies to support the false story. As we string more lies together, we increase the odds we will be caught in them. Once this happens, we lose control of the narrative and the fallout.

Intentional lying and its exposure will generate a devastating consequence: loss of trust. A web of deception undermines and diminishes trust, changing the dynamics within relationships. This shift might have begun in subtle ways but becomes unmistakable to the other person once lies are exposed. On some level the other person recognizes that our decision to lie to them means we devalue them.

The consequence of this breach can vary. At times, a single lie can irreparably destroy the trust in a relationship; no assertion of regret or commitment of future trustworthiness will be believed and the relationship cannot be sustained. In other cases, outward effects might not seem evident at all. But in most every case, the distrust following exposure of deception leads to relationships where interactions are more superficial and guarded and less honest and vulnerable.

> The distrust following exposure of deception leads to relationships where interactions are more superficial and guarded and less honest and vulnerable.

Sadly, this diminishing trust relationship may become our norm. None of us are immune to the seduction of deceptiveness—in large and small ways we are naturally inclined toward practicing this toward others and having it done to us. Deception becomes so common in our relationships with others and in their relationships with us that we just factor it into all our interactions. "Trust but verify" becomes the rule. Although this stance might protect us from exploitation or disappointment, it also produces shallow trust and correspondingly shallow relationships. We are left more isolated and vulnerable even as deceptiveness renders impossible the trusting dance of giving, receiving, and giving again.

This diminishment of trust and its consequences reveal we have once again come full circle with our attempts to avoid vulnerability. As with dominating fear and grasping fear, hiding and lying expressions of fear only add to our sense of vulnerability. The apparent futility of these efforts leads us to what may be the core expression of destructive fear: god-like control. In the next chapter we will consider controlling expressions of destructive fear.

Questions for Reflection

1. How have your own knowledge and imagination been collaborators in your life? Give examples of how you have combined these and created new solutions when confronting old challenges.
2. How have the burdens of "keeping up appearances" impacted your life and relationships? What might happen if you let those burdens go?
3. What messages have you received about the appropriateness (or inappropriateness) of particular feelings? How have these messages helped (or hindered) in maintaining trusting relationships with yourself and others?
4. Have you or someone you have known become trapped by a web of lies that became harder and harder to maintain? How did the deception impact interconnected relationships?

A Window from Scripture

The Story of Human Creation and Fall
(Gen. 2:7-9, 15-18, 22-25; 3:1-9)

This faith story of human beginnings paints a picture of the original harmony of the human family with the creation; the human disrespect for the Creator's limits; and the subsequent disharmony, distrust, and fear resulting from this fateful choice. More than a parable, it holds up a mirror reflecting the experience of every human living in a world where distrust and fear now rule.

> Then the Lord God formed man from the dust of the ground, and breathed into his nostrils the breath of life; and the man became a living being. And the Lord God planted a garden in Eden, in the east; and there he put the man whom he had formed. Out of the ground the Lord God made to grow every tree that is pleasant to the sight and good for food, the tree of life also in the midst of the garden, and the tree of the knowledge of good and evil.
>
> The Lord God took the man and put him in the garden of Eden to till it and keep it. And the Lord God commanded the man, "You may freely eat of every tree of the garden; but of the tree of the knowledge of good and evil you shall not eat, for in the day that you eat of it you shall die."
>
> Then the Lord God said, "It is not good that the man should be alone; I will make him a helper as his partner."
>
> And the rib that the Lord God had taken from the man he made into a woman and brought her to the man. Then the man said, "This at last is bone of my bones and flesh of my flesh; this one shall be called Woman, for out of Man this one was taken." Therefore a man leaves his father and his mother and clings to his wife, and they become one flesh. And the man and his wife were both naked, and were not ashamed.
>
> Now the serpent was more crafty than any other wild animal that the Lord God had made. He said to the woman, "Did God say, 'You shall not eat from any tree in the garden'?" The woman said to the serpent, "We may eat of the fruit of the trees in the garden; but God said, 'You shall not eat of the fruit of the tree that is in the middle of the garden, nor shall you touch it, or you shall die.'" But the serpent said to the woman, "You will not die; for God knows that when you eat of it your eyes will

be opened, and you will be like God, knowing good and evil." So when the woman saw that the tree was good for food, and that it was a delight to the eyes, and that the tree was to be desired to make one wise, she took of its fruit and ate; and she also gave some to her husband, who was with her, and he ate. Then the eyes of both were opened, and they knew that they were naked; and they sewed fig leaves together and made loincloths for themselves.

They heard the sound of the Lord God walking in the garden at the time of the evening breeze, and the man and his wife hid themselves from the presence of the Lord God among the trees of the garden. But the Lord God called to the man, and said to him, "Where are you?"

This faith story from Genesis 2 and 3 is a parallel account to the faith story found in Genesis 1:26-31a (which was touched upon in Chapter 1). Both of these faith stories portray a giving Creator who brings all things into existence with care, intention, and purpose while demonstrating a special relationship with humanity. The previously discussed story highlights humanity's likeness to the Giving Creator; humanity is made in the Creator's image, receives the blessing of fruitfulness, and is given authority over the rest of creation.

This second story grounds humanity within creation. In an earthy, personal, and intimate way, the Lord God forms the man from the dust of the ground and breathes into his nostrils the breath of life. In another act of tenderness, the Lord God removes the man's rib while he is sleeping and uses this body part closest to his most vital organs to make the woman. Their own intimacy, vulnerability, and security are described in the words, "And the man and his wife were both naked, and were not ashamed."

Included in the gifts of the Creator was the tree of the knowledge of good and evil that stood in the middle of the garden. With its forbidden fruit, it gave the man and woman opportunity to reveal the depth of their trust in the Giving Creator. Having already received life, companionship, and meaningful work through the trusting acts of the Creator, would they in response trust their Giver and respect the one and only limiting boundary they were given?

Unfortunately, their response revealed the shallowness of their trust. They listened to the skeptical and untrustworthy words of the crafty serpent. Desiring the forbidden wisdom, "god-like" knowledge, and hoped-for control that might be obtained through distrusting the trustworthy Giving Creator, the woman ate some of the fruit and gave some to her husband who also ate it.

Immediately, this act of distrust opened their eyes to a new world of distrustfulness all around them. The trust between the man and the woman, between these human creatures and the Giving Creator, and between these human creatures and the creation they lived in was irreparably changed. The once-interdependent harmony of the creation was thrown into unresolvable conflict as distrust was sown into every nook and cranny of the creation. No longer anchored in trust, the human couple had no landmarks they could use in orienting themselves or helping them pinpoint their location in their new world. They were lost. The Lord God's haunting question, "Where are you?" was not so much a query about their physical whereabouts but a deeper question about who and where they were now in relation to themselves, each other, the creation, and their Creator.

How would they now navigate this new world of unleashed fear where distrust, dis-ease, and discord seemed as natural as breathing?

In this faith story, the couples covered their awareness of vulnerability with fig leaves, but this provided little comfort when the Lord God came walking through the garden. Our own efforts to cover ourselves fare no better. After all, how effectively have dominating, grasping, and lying strategies reduced our feelings of exposure and vulnerability? Why might we think we would get a different result from pooling these strategies together and exercising a god-like control over others and ourselves? Though experience might teach us otherwise, the lure of controlling power and knowledge continues to beckon us with its false promises. What happens when we, like the first human couple, are seduced by its attractions?

Chapter 5
Turning the Gift of Limited Choice into Controlling Fear

Searching for Control

Being human is an amazing gift! Perhaps the highest expression of that gift is choice-making capacity and the exercise of decisional will. Blending the gifts of conscious awareness, imagination, and knowledge, we formulate options and alternatives, consider and evaluate their merits, and make definitive choices. When we make use of this choice-making capacity and choose to practice trust, we can freely participate in the Giving Creator's intended dance of giving, receiving, and giving again with trust.

Nevertheless, limitation constrains our choices. Limited security, limited resources, and *limited knowledge* together bring *limited choice*. When viewing these limitations as gifts of the Creator, they become pathways for deepening trust and community. Unfortunately, the more common perception is viewing these as reminders of human vulnerability and ongoing impediments to freedom. This latter viewpoint fosters both resistance to limitations and avoidance of feelings of vulnerability. As this view is translated into action, it unleashes destructive fear, nurturing the many expressions of fear that naturally follow.

This unleashing of fear comes easily. Like Adam and Eve in the faith story, we can give in to the temptation—we disrespect and resist the real limits of the Creator. As we follow this enticing desire, we feed an appetite for a god-like experience of power and control. This temptation might promise a greater sense of security and an intoxicating mastering of one's own destiny, but it brings neither security nor mastery. Instead, it unleashes a host of destructive behaviors that rob, distort, and bring pain.

These are unintended effects. We would not set out to practice dominating behaviors and the hurtful, depersonalizing words and actions that are so destructive in relationships. Nor would we start with the intent of holding so tightly to what we have and harboring suspiciousness of the motives of others. We would not begin with an intention of deceiving others and ourselves with distortive lies that hide the truth of our vulnerability and limitation.

But the unleashing of destructive fear draws out all these behaviors. They are natural reactions to the unlimited insecurity, unlimited wants, and unlimited capacity to lie that routinely follow our choice of living outside the real but safer boundaries given by the Creator. Fear's unleashing is a problem. Once the genie is out of the bottle, we cannot put it back.

Like Adam and Eve, we humans have the capacity with our willful choice to unleash destructive fear; we do not have the capacity within ourselves to reverse the effects of this decision and return to the Creator's original intended dance of giving, receiving, and giving again with trust. In a painful irony, the very real limits of limited security, limited resources, limited knowledge, and limited choice—originally given to keep us safe—also bind us to the distorting effects of destructive fear. These real limits keep us from mustering the necessary security, resources, knowledge, and array of choices needed to change our situation. Instead, like an infectious disease for which we have no cure, destructive fear spreads in us, among us, and through us to rob, kill, and destroy.

> Like an infectious disease for which we have no cure, destructive fear spreads in us, among us, and through us to rob, kill, and destroy.

Despite this, we will keep trying to manage the fear and control its damage. Our lack of ability to control these effects only intensifies our desire to subdue their many expressions. *Controlling fear* is born.

Redoubling our efforts, we pursue futile strategies for the very control we cannot achieve. Our original disrespect for real limits may have created destructive fear but we engage in the same disrespect for limits as we try regaining control over it with controlling fear. Magnifying and extending the distortions of all the other forms of destructive fear, expressions of controlling fear promise protection from the damaging effects of destructive fear but actually trap us ever more deeply in its clutches.

Strategies for Internal Control

The simplest internally focused controlling strategy is "negative willpower"—resolving not to do a particular action or behavior. Negative willpower uses the power of our own wills, focusing on exterminating or avoiding what we do not want to do. We individually set the goal, we muster the resources, and we individually determine what constitutes success in meeting the goal. Using this willpower, we focus attention on objectives like not thinking lustful thoughts, on resisting our greed, or quashing any rising of pride.

"Negative willpower" might appear to be a promising strategy but it reveals the opposite in actual practice. It sows the seeds of its own failure. Focusing on not doing a particular action or behavior actually makes the action seem more attractive, desirable, and therefore more difficult to resist. Concentrating more intently on avoiding lustful thoughts makes these thoughts more enticing. Trying to limit greed makes us want even more. If we start subduing pride, we are soon seduced by a pride in our newfound humility. In almost every case, our human capacity for self-deception and self-sabotage quickly undermines any temporary success.

A controlling strategy a notch above simple willpower is the establishment and following of rules. Rules can be quite beneficial. Rules, even when self-chosen, offer an external viewpoint that gives them more objective authority. They serve a useful purpose by offering shorthand for evaluating potential courses of action, eliminating a need for carefully considering the merits of every little decision. Rules give us time-proven principles, informing the best course of action. For example, truth telling might be one principled rule we would choose to follow. If I am relying on this rule, my decision will be simplified by the automatic elimination of a host of untruthful options.

But rules do not stand by themselves. Motivating them is some centering authority, encouraging us to keep them. When we formulate rules centered on respect for the real limits given by the Creator, we are operating within the intended values of the Creator. The healthy fear generated corresponds to the real limits that already exist. Trusting in the Giver of limits, this fear persuades non-coercively, encouraging the keeping of the rule. Healthy (reality-based) fear simplifies decision-making, bringing the freedom to give, receive, and give again with trust.

> Healthy, reality-based fear simplifies decision-making, bringing the freedom to give, receive, and give again with trust.

When we resist real limits and unleash controlling fear, we change the motivating center, propelling us into a world of insecurity—rule making and rule keeping get distorted. Controlling fear replaces healthy fear. Rules become tools used for imposing control as we try to rein in the unwanted effects of living outside the safe boundaries of real limits.

The initial thrust of this now-distorted rule making and rule keeping focuses on asserting internal control over our own attitudes and behaviors. We establish personal rules for the behaviors or attitudes we desire to control. Before long, these strictly individual efforts fall short. Even with the best of intentions, self-chosen rules alone offer little likelihood of maintaining compliance.

To fill the gaps, we reinforce our personal rules with rules carrying the wisdom of community experience. Sometimes, time-honored rules like the "Ten Commandments" or a list like the "Seven Deadly Sins" (anger, lust, greed, gluttony, envy, sloth, and pride) can give direction, using peer pressure to strengthen our resolve. But any positive results here are temporary, often producing instead a resentment-filled, compliant obedience. As we observe with "negative will-power," the making of a rule only makes its violation more enticing. When the rule says, "No you won't," a resistant part of us may reply, "Yes I will."

This should not surprise us. "Rule" is just another name for a limitation. If we were already willing to violate the real limits of the Creator, would we expect better compliance with self or community made rules? With controlling fear generating the rules, negative consequences become necessary to compel compliance. Even when we might not respect the rule itself, we may still comply to avoid the undesired consequence.

Options for negative consequences might include a physical infliction of pain, temporary confinement, reduction of privileges or withholding of sources of pleasure. Another penalty might include the pronouncement of guilt and attendant shaming responses from other individuals, the community, or even our own selves. The negative consequence may fall on a spectrum anywhere from a mere disapproving frown for a minor offense to life imprisonment or execution for the most heinous crimes. Compelling compliance requires the consequence to be perceived as sufficiently discouraging and unpleasant. It must also manufacture enough accompanying fear to overcome any fear-inspired resistance to keeping the rule. Once controlling fear is unleashed, a rule-based orientation requires an ever-present fear to remain effective.

This development establishes controlling fear, in all its coercive, destructive, and distortive power, as the norm. We trap ourselves in a self-created bind, leaving us little freedom or choice. If we keep these self-chosen rules, we are shackled to a compliant but resistant obedience, cowering fearfully, avoiding unwanted consequences. If we choose to resist and disobey the rules, we are shackled to the fear-based consequences we anticipate or receive. Either way, we are held in bondage with no way of escape. Rule-making and rule-keeping ultimately achieve the opposite of their intent. We may intend them to bring control, but they actually leave us more out of control.

> Rule-making and rule-keeping ultimately achieve the opposite of their intent.
> We may intend them to bring control;
> they actually leave us more out of control.

This failure and futility of self-chosen rules can provoke another set of controlling strategies: medication and distraction. With these, we continue maintaining the illusion of internal control while looking for things outside ourselves that can both deflect our attention from our insecurity and try to fill an empty hole in our psyche. Abusing alcohol or drugs might provide the most obvious example of this self-medication but there is a seemingly endless list of potential medicating mediums. Food, relationships, sex, and work—all good gifts given for enriching our lives within the boundaries of their original purpose—can each be misused and distorted in an endless pursuit of distraction and addiction. Similarly, religion, sports, exercise, shopping, cooking, social media, and general busyness—all activities demonstrating our human creativity—can mindlessly distract us from being aware of a lack of security, meaning, and purpose in our lives. Medicating and distracting strategies do little to generate real and lasting security.

All these futile controlling strategies only numb us, insulating us from experiencing and recognizing its real source: destructive fear. Just as a fish would be unaware of the water around it because water is integral to its life and existence, we can eventually lose any consciousness of the many forms of destructive fear because they are so ingrained in our experience of the world around us. Living unaware can become the only "living" we know; fear is then freed to continue its distortive, destructive work, bringing a miserable and meaningless existence. Remaining unnamed and out of awareness, the power of this fear continues unchecked.

This may be a miserable existence, but it is possible to stay medicated and distracted, mindlessly subsisting—merely surviving—from one day to the next. We can avoid silence, intimacy, mortality, and anything else exposing our neediness, vulnerability, or lack of control. Sadly, some people in our culture continue on this futile path, trying to block out the gnawing consciousness of vulnerability lying just outside the periphery of our awareness. Whether with the previously discussed failures of dominating, grasping, and lying strategies or our best efforts at distracting, medicating and avoiding, this threat of vulnerability always seems to remain with us—a haunting presence.

Seeking External Control and Finding a "god" of Fear

At its core, disrespecting and defying the limits of the Creator—the original decision creating destructive fear—expresses a desire for internal control and freedom from external constraints. We can pursue all these internal strategies—negative willpower, rule-making and rule-keeping, medication and distraction—while maintaining the illusion that we are using them to stay in control. The opposite is true, however. These soon demonstrate our lack of control, reminding us we are not in charge. This fruitless pursuit of internal control actually reaps a harvest of meaninglessness and a more confining bondage. We stay stuck, whether we realize it or not. We do not have the power or resources within ourselves to change our basic vulnerability.

As these strategies of internal control prove insufficient, external sources of control become more attractive—we start looking beyond ourselves for assistance, hoping to find the security that eludes us. Although we may not completely abandon our efforts at internal control, we join with others in hopes that our personal sense of vulnerability can be protected by a greater security within our wider community.

Some initial steps into external control can be seen in societal pressures to pass more laws, increase police forces and prison populations, expand military capabilities, and exert moral and religious prohibitions. In each of these, the wider community is assembling resources in a focused response to this need for feeling more secure. At best, these constraints offer only a temporary sense of safety. We still remain troubled by the gnawing awareness that we are trading the loss of more personal freedom for an elusive, but ultimately unobtainable security.

Despite these community efforts and our personal efforts to convince ourselves otherwise, the unrelieved anxiety persists. Neediness and vulnerability still haunt us—individually and collectively. The depth of this anxiety makes space for a more radical leap: imaging an external power, a "god," capable of protecting vulnerability and neediness while offering invulnerability and absolute sufficiency in their place.

As an answer to human anxiety, this humanly imaged "god" brings a paradoxical shift. Human imagination creates this external power while anticipating being subject to this humanly created "power." Furthermore, though deriving its power from human imagination, this "god" possesses power far beyond human capabilities. Making use of this creative paradox, our human imaginations seek the reassuring safety we hope to find as we align ourselves with this "god's" imagined power. We look for this "power" to save us from the very real vulnerability and neediness that terrify us.

This "product" of human imagination exacts a heavy price from its human creators. Unlike the strictly human collective efforts to fashion security—adding laws, expanding police forces and prisons, and imposing moral and religious prohibitions—this imaging of external power creates a "god"—the ultimate maker and enforcer of rules. This "god" subjects its human creators to its authority and control. Individually or collectively, we can choose to disbelieve in or resist the authority of this imagination-created "being," but once created in the collective mind of humanity, it cannot be ignored. This humanly created "god" becomes a measuring rod against which we humans define and understand our own selves and the world in which we live—whether we believe in it or not.

> This humanly created "god" becomes a measuring rod against which we humans define and understand our own selves and the world in which we live—whether we believe in it or not.

With imaginations already tainted by the controlling expressions of destructive fear, we humans would naturally imagine a "power" shaped by fear and not bound by the limits constraining humanity. This imaged "god" would embody all the values of destructive fear—only with greater power and knowledge. This "god" would be invulnerable and all-powerful, lacking nothing and possessing all things, be unknowably hidden and know all things, be subject to nothing and controlling all things.

Wielding coercive power as it is grasping, hiding, and controlling, this imaged "god" might offer some semblance of security. Might not aligning ourselves (or at least maintaining a fearful compliance) with the desires of this "god" help us reestablish the sense of control we seek, securing us from our personal dread of vulnerability? We might wish this were so, but any security within this alignment would always be shaky. This humanly created "god" would not be so freely managed, manipulated, or controlled by its human creators. By its own definition, it would instead be free to turn against us at any moment for any reason and wreak its destructiveness upon us. A fear-created "god" would have little reason to cater to our desires.

Knowing this, how could this kind of "god" have any viability in human thought or practice? Would we not recognize the inherent insecurity brought by this humanly created image and reject it? Not necessarily. As a practicing Christian, I recognize that many aspects and characteristics attributed to this humanly imaged "god" closely resemble an image of God presented by many people to be the God of the Bible. In biblical texts, the word "fear" is used in reference to God hundreds of times in phrases such as "Fear God," "Fear the LORD," and "The fear of the LORD." Many interpreters understand these passages to describe a fear more akin to sheer terror where the presence of God evokes profound shame, guilt, and insecurity.

If we are viewing significant portions of the biblical record through a particular interpretive lens—destructive fear—we could easily find a "god" who demands absolute obedience and exacts punishment on those who fail to comply. Viewed through this lens, humanity is placed in the role of "walking on eggshells" to avoid violating some law and unleashing a god-attributed wrath that can swallow up even the ignorant and innocent in its wake.

Some readers might be troubled by my connecting this "god" of human imagination with common interpretations of the God of the Bible. It was initially troubling for me. But the words of biblical texts support this linking as long as destructive fear is guiding our understanding of them.

This troubling connection need not surprise us. Destructive fear distorts perception everywhere. Anytime we see biblical interpretations where coercive, controlling, and dominating power is being invoked in the name of God, we would be wise to question whether distortions of destructive fear might be at work. Fear's distortive effect on sacred writings is not unique to Christian scriptures. Any religious or spiritual framework can be hijacked by the distortions of a fear-tainted interpretation.

> Any religious or spiritual framework can be hijacked by the distortions of a fear-tainted interpretation.

Recognizing this possibility, the humanly created "god" of fear can become problematic on several levels. First of all, it does not answer the need for greater security but only adds to our insecurity. If violating our self-chosen rules might bring on unpleasant consequences, these would certainly pale in comparison to the potential eternal consequences we might attribute to crossing this "god" of fear. How secure would we be if we are living in constant dread that an errant thought or action might draw the wrath of this all-knowing and all-powerful "god"? If we believe this "god" exists, we must either cower constantly in fear or further medicate and distract ourselves from the doom that is sure to come—or both.

Second, this humanly created "god" represents and reflects distorted values that cannot sustain our living and our relationships over time. Just as with all "gods," the characteristics and powers we attribute to this "god" will mirror what is most important to us. The unlimited power we ascribe to this "god" reflects the power and knowledge we covet and wish for ourselves. Conceiving a "god" of self-contained invulnerability, all-sufficiency, hiddenness, and control highlights that we treasure the power to avoid vulnerability, neediness, disclosure, and unmanageability. This yearning for unlimited power and the desire for avoiding limitation are two sides of the same coin. Both sides of this coin set in motion and perpetuate all the behaviors and attitudes of destructive fear, destroying trust and security in each of our relationships.

Attributing these values to a "god" we would then "worship" also sets up a self-reinforcing loop that continually confirms these trust-destroying values—validating our exercising them in our relationships. If the "god" I worship affirms these values, surely this allows me to justify any actions I might practice that would be consistent with these values. As we keep following this destructive logic, we can freely exercise all the dominating, grasping, lying, and controlling expressions of destructive fear without the burdening constraints of conscience—especially when we do them in the service of our "god."

A third problem flows naturally out of the second one. If our highest desires are possessing unlimited power or avoiding limitedness—the values of this humanly imaged "god"—then we are encouraged to define the world around us and our own selves by how well we muster power for ourselves or avoid evidences of our limitedness. This definition naturally sets up a constant drumbeat of comparison. Do we have more power and more stuff than our neighbors? Are we less exposed and more in control? This prompting toward comparison does little toward building relationships of trust and security. If my personal sense of value is defined by how I compare to those around me, I have every incentive to manipulate and use others for my own benefit while undermining and sabotaging their every effort. Unfortunately, whether acknowledging it or not, when we have this orientation, we create together a world filled with violence, distrust, deception, and coercion.

> If my personal sense of value is defined by how I compare to those around me, I have every incentive to manipulate and use others for my own benefit while undermining and sabotaging their every effort.

The result is the ultimate ironic twist. We start down this path into destructive fear by defying the limits of the Creator in hopes of gaining freedom unconstrained by the bounds of human limitation. Disrespecting the safer boundaries of real limitation, we seek a god-like experience of power, control, and the mastery of our own destiny. Despite all these efforts, we do not find what we are seeking. This ill-chosen path unleashes destructive fear into our lives and relationships instead. This fear brings an ever-present sensitivity to undesired vulnerability, provoking never-ending efforts at managing its effects. In this life-diminishing process, we can impose rules with fearful consequences and various strategies of medication and distraction. Eventually, we look in desperation for a "god" of fear—created in the human imagination—for bringing both an ally in the enforcement of fear-based rules and a protective power against the haunting vulnerability and neediness.

This is where the road ends. Neither the destructive fear created by defying human limitation nor aligning ourselves with a humanly created "god" of fear leads to any kind of lasting security. Fear's distortions leave us robbed of hope and meaning. The end of this road is a dead end.

With this ironic twist we wind up with what we most dread—a world where vulnerability is exposed and exploited—and all we can do is live in the emptiness and insecurity of destructive fear. No wonder we would deny, distract, medicate, and do anything imaginable to numb our awareness to the truth of our plight. Destructive fear leaves us lost—truly lost—with seemingly nowhere left to turn.

Questions for Reflection

1. What has been your experience with "negative willpower"? How has it worked out for you or for others you have known?
2. How has rule making and rule keeping been helpful to you? How have these created problems in your life or in your relationships?
3. How have "medication and distraction" impacted you personally or the lives of those around you?
4. How has your own understanding of God been shaped by images filled with fear? How have these images influenced your capacity for trusting yourself, others, and God?

A Window from Scripture

The Parable of Two Lost Sons
(Luke 15:11-13, 17-25, 28-32)

This parable, commonly known as "The Parable of the Prodigal Son," is probably the most familiar one told by Jesus. A more accurate title would be "The Parable of the Two Lost Sons," but the story focuses on the loving father—the Giver of grace. This father, who represents the Giving Creator in the story, gives freely with little regard for the worthiness of the recipients.

> Then Jesus said, "There was a man who had two sons. The younger of them said to his father, 'Father, give me the share of the property that will belong to me.' So he divided his property between them. A few days later the younger son gathered all he had and traveled to a distant country, and there he squandered his property in dissolute living... But when he came to himself he said, 'How many of my father's hired hands have bread enough and to spare, but here I am dying of hunger! I will get up and go to my father, and I will say to him, "Father, I have sinned against heaven and before you; I am no longer worthy to be called your son; treat me like one of your hired hands."' So he set off and went to his father. But while he was still far off, his father saw him and was filled with compassion; he ran and put his arms around him and kissed him. Then the son said to him, 'Father, I have sinned against heaven and before you; I am no longer worthy to be called your son.' But the father said to his slaves, 'Quickly, bring out a robe—the best one—and put it on him; put a ring on his finger and sandals on his feet. And get the fatted calf and kill it, and let us eat and celebrate; for this son of mine was dead and is alive again; he was lost and is found!' And they began to celebrate.
>
> "Now his elder son was in the field; and when he came and approached the house, he heard music and dancing. . . . Then he became angry and refused to go in. His father came out and began to plead with him. But he answered his father, 'Listen! For all these years I have been working like a slave for you, and I have never disobeyed your command; yet you have never given me even a young goat so that I might celebrate with my friends. But when this son of yours came back, who has devoured your

property with prostitutes, you killed the fatted calf for him!' Then the father said to him, 'Son, you are always with me, and all that is mine is yours. But we had to celebrate and rejoice, because this brother of yours was dead and has come to life; he was lost and has been found.'"

This story follows two parables of lost things—a lost sheep and a lost coin—and tells the story of two sons who are lost. Their lostness comes as they forget their relationship with the Giver and cling instead to a possessive relationship with the gifts of the Giver. In their misperception, they define their sonship by the material trappings that accrue to them as sons rather than the relationship with the father providing them. In their eyes, their father is only an object—the means toward an end—the potential supplier for meeting their desires. They reveal their lostness through their actions.

The younger son demonstrates his lostness by leaving home. In a gesture of "you are already dead to me," he prematurely claims the material portion of his inheritance, taking what he newly possesses to a distant country—far away from his father, his brother, and any likeness to the son he was intended to be. He completes the disrespect for his father and himself by squandering all he has received in wild and unrestrained existence.

The older son lives out his lostness without ever leaving home. He dutifully works each day with a resentful but outwardly compliant obedience. One can easily imagine his jealous speculations about his younger brother's activities and the pride-filled sense of superiority he nurtures, keeping his own demons at bay. Unlike the younger son, he holds tightly to his inheritance, diligently working to expand what he understands it to be. Like the younger son, he focuses on the material trappings to the exclusion of his relationship with his father or his brother.

Initially sharing lostness, the two sons respond differently as the story continues. The younger son recognizes the misery of his situation. Humbled and vulnerable, he resolves to return to a relationship with the father—no longer as a son but in hopes of being received as a mere servant. He could never have imagined the loving, grace-filled response he actually receives.

The father does not even wait for him to get home. He sees his wayward son at a distance, running to him, embracing him, and kissing him. Calling urgently for servants to bring the best robe, a ring, and sandals—all outward signs of sonship—the father throws a party of welcome and celebration.

This younger son, once lost in his own self-deceptive arrogance, greed, and disrespect, is now a son who has been found. With a heart open to and changed by transforming grace, this younger son is no longer dead to his true sonship. Now he is truly alive in the grace-filled relationship with the father.

From the perspective of grace, there can be no greater joy. The one who was lost has been found. This loving grace does not define him by his choices of the past but frees him, making possible the life-giving relationship the Giver intended for him with his father, his brother, and the world at large. The grace-gift of the loving father set in motion a renewal of the dance of giving, receiving, and giving again with trust.

The older son has a different response to the loving grace of the father. He remains lost. He sees unfairness in grace. In his mind and heart, the appropriate response to his wayward biological relation would have been pronouncing guilt, shaming the offender, and rendering a retaliatory rejection. Seeing the gracing of the father only aggravates this older son's growing anger and resentment. Referencing "this son of yours," he disowns his relationship with his brother and chooses to remain outside the loving grace the father would gladly extend to him.

This response of the older son serves as a reminder that grace does not coerce its response. The resistant heart might even be hardened by grace. But for an open heart, grace can bring healing and restoration for the past and present, making possible a loving and grace-filled hope for the future. Will grace find our hearts open to its transforming, healing power?

* I use LOVE (all caps) to denote the indescribable love characterizing and coming from the Creator. I use love (lower case) to describe the human love that sometimes mirrors LOVE.

Chapter 6
Being Found
by the Giver of LOVE

Being Found by Love

Being human is an amazing gift! Destructive fear robs us of many of the benefits of this gift and gets us lost. All the dominating, grasping, lying, and controlling expressions of destructive fear separate us further from the gift of our humanity and from the Creator's intended dance of giving, receiving, and giving again in trust. We may get so lost that we may be unable to see gift, Giver, or the possibility they could exist. Like the younger son in the parable Jesus told, our choices may have left us trapped in a country far removed from our Creator's original intention and purpose. We may wonder, "Can I return, and if so, how?"

A return from the far country may seem impossible. Everything we learn from destructive fear denies it. Fear avoids neediness and vulnerability, cultivating coercive power and fostering distrust. Destructive fear deceives us, telling us that any admission of lostness only increases the likelihood of exploitation and further wounding. Furthermore, fear cannot make sense of grace and love. These appear to be undermining the fear-inspired goal of acquiring more security. Would grace and love not make us more insecure?

As humans, we naturally pay more attention to things that confirm our preconceptions and overlook those that challenge them. It's easy to continue giving weight and credibility to destructive fear and the "god" of fear that personifies it—despite ongoing awareness of the pitfalls. We diminish grace and love, portraying them as only lofty ideals offering little to the real world. This "logic" from destructive fear rules them out, discouraging any hope of being freed from the clutches of fear.

Destructive fear also distorts memory of the Giving Creator. As fear discounts the value of grace and love, it also induces forgetfulness of the God who embodies grace and healing love. Despite this forgetfulness, there is a faith-filled memory telling us that this Giving Creator is still the giver of life, consciousness, and imagination along with the original will and freedom to make choices. There is a faith telling us that our forgetfulness or any resistance we might have in trusting this God does not change this gracing God's stance toward us. Immeasurably different in character and purpose from a "god" of fear, this forgotten Creator God always was and always is truly a God of healing LOVE.

> Immeasurably different in character and purpose from a "god" of fear, the forgotten Creator God always was and always is truly a God of healing LOVE.

Jesus' parable of the loving father offers a new and personal glimpse of the Creator God of LOVE. This God, revealed in the loving father, is not dominating, grasping, hidden, or controlling in responses. The younger son's forgetfulness of his original heritage is not met with rejection or demands for restitution. Instead, this God initiates with open-armed grace and non-coercive LOVE, delighting in renewed opportunities for rejoining the dance of giving, receiving, and giving again with trust. Unlike his child's self-willed forgetfulness, this loving father remembers—not to punish or chastise, but to restore and renew. The Creator God of LOVE revealed in this story turns the values of destructive fear upside down (or more accurately, "right side up").

When we are immersed in fear, this "right side up" healing LOVE may feel strange and foreign. To our distorted senses, destructive fear seems to be the original, preeminent, and normal way to experience the world. Fear's opposite—LOVE—appears to be its inferior and abnormal counter. But if we jog our memories, we discover this distorted perception of reality is what is actually turned around. Remembering again the original faith story of the Giving Creator and the creation, we remind ourselves that the qualities of this healing LOVE have been present from the beginning and came before fear. When our memories are restored, LOVE is setting the norm and fear is the distortive imposter. Destructive fear and the imposter "god" of fear we humans have created reflect the complete opposite of the true Giving Creator's character and original intention.

The Giving Creator is characterized by LOVE, but the word "love" can be used in many ways. I might say, "I 'love' my spouse," "I 'love' my home," "I 'love' my outfit," or "I 'love' this cookie." Though I may be using the same word "love" in each phrase, the depth and meaning I attach to "love" may be falling on a continuum anywhere from a life-long commitment to a passing whim. If LOVE is the very nature of the Creator God and foundation upon which the whole creation is built, how then do we recognize this LOVE and distinguish it from its lesser substitutes? After all, much of what we may be calling "love" contains a grasping spirit and possessiveness triggered by the insecurities of destructive fear.

Describing LOVE
(Part 1)

This healing LOVE that characterizes the Giving Creator God is described in the biblical text of 1 Corinthians 13. It is the same love the father in Jesus' parable embodied to his two sons. These oft-quoted words are almost too familiar, hindering our recognition of the radical distinctiveness and practical significance of LOVE.

In 1 Corinthians 13: 4-6, we read: "Love is patient; love is kind; love is not envious or boastful or arrogant or rude. It does not insist on its own way: it is not irritable or resentful; it does not rejoice in wrongdoing, but rejoices in the truth." This list in 1 Corinthians 13 begins with two affirmations of what LOVE is and ends with an affirmation of what LOVE does. In between, the passage distinguishes LOVE from actions and attitudes that are often distorted expressions of what is called "love." LOVE is patient and kind. Patience is willing to wait, and kindness is unwilling to resort to hurtful actions to get its way. Both of these offer a sharp contrast to typical fear-based actions.

One appeal of fear-based behaviors is the quick and demonstrable results they bring. In the short term, I can easily manipulate others into doing what I want by using dominating and controlling tactics. Longer-term results of impatience may not bode well for the rest of the world or for me. Resentments spawned by manipulated compliance produce destructive reactions, generating further manipulations that are passed on to others or directed back at me. Unkindness, in similar fashion, hurts people; people who are hurt, in turn, hurt more people. In the end, both impatience and unkindness close doors of relational connection and narrow opportunities for growing trust.

> Impatience and unkindness close doors of relational connection and narrow opportunities for growing trust.

Patience and kindness expand opportunity and possibility, creating a safety zone that promotes collaboration and new possibilities. If I can trust that others will be patient and kind in their assessment of me, then I am free to devote myself fully to the situation at hand without fear of a negative judgment stifling my creativity. This can be especially freeing when I am extending this same patience and kindness in my own self-assessments. How many times are we our own most impatient and unkind critics? Fostering an environment where we are freely functioning in this zone of safety fills our lives and the lives of those around us with new meaning and creativity. When patience and kindness grow, they enrich and fulfill the lives of both the giver and receiver of these gifts of LOVE.

If we were relying solely on logical processes, we would practice patience and kindness as the obvious choice in almost any situation. These clearly offer the better long-term approach. Despite this reality, our personal choices and the choices of others may not reflect the simple wisdom of this logic. Our predisposition is making choices driven by short-term needs or fears. This preference demonstrates just how vulnerable we are to the short-term demands of destructive fear and our lack of trust in the longer-term benefits of waiting. Breaking this pattern and disarming fear require our awareness and the intentional embracing of healing LOVE qualities such as patience and kindness.

Following this affirmation of patience and kindness, the familiar list focuses on eight distorted expressions that do not constitute LOVE. All of them may sometimes be associated with some aspect of being "loving," but each is still a destructive distortion of LOVE. The first three of these are envy, boasting, and arrogance (pride); each of these is a distortion of the love of self. They all begin with valuations we make about others and ourselves based on comparisons generated by the insecurities of destructive fear. Fearing harsh judgments from those fear-inspired comparisons, we use these tools, attempting to protect our self-image.

Envy attempts protection by watching resentfully toward what others have received; it both desires what the other has and is unhappy that they have it. With envy, I take no joy in others' enjoyment of good things because I so resent not having them for myself. Even more, my own joy in what I have is diminished when I see others enjoying what I do not have. This distorted self-love found in envy might be summed up in the phrase, "If I can't have it, no one can."

In actuality, envy does not protect at all; it inhibits the experiencing of grace. Envy diminishes my appreciation of my own gifts, and my self-absorbed resentments can have a spoiling effect on the gifts of others. In short, envy shrinks the pie for all of us. Healing LOVE does not envy: it enlarges possibilities, opening up new pathways for grace to enter our lives and the lives of others.

> Healing LOVE does not envy: it enlarges possibilities, opening up new pathways for grace to enter our lives and the lives of others.

Boasting tries to build me up at the expense of others. I brag and exaggerate the significance of my gifts and attributes while belittling and minimizing the gifts of others. I project an air of superiority in hopes of raising the perception of my own relative standing. At the same time, I use my boasting to diminish the relative standing of the other—often by humiliating them in the exchange.

While attempts at inflating my image may illustrate the more familiar form of boasting, there is an equally destructive flipside: I can "boast" of my inferiority relative to others. Though these might appear to be opposites, they both serve a similar purpose. Inflating my projected image or deflating that image can both be attempts at making me stand out in the crowd. With both I avoid the more dreaded fate of not being noticed at all. Boasting reflects my insecurities about my value and the value of the unique gifts I have received. Even though boasting might offer me short-term comfort, over time it damages the base of trust with self and others that is necessary for authentic life-giving relationships.

Arrogance (pride), while grouped with envy and boasting in the list of 1 Corinthians, moves well beyond them. Like envy and boasting, pride starts with a comparative stance rooted in destructive fear. It grows into a state of being that is resistant to recognizing any need for change or transformation.

Unlike pride, envy and boasting can be distinguished as behaviors we do. An underlying sense of insecurity and inadequacy fuels them. As a result, we may continue acting out both of them even as we know on some level that they are based on unsustainable beliefs.

With pride, we come to believe our own lies. Our insecurities are suppressed by a denial-based confidence in our self-satisfied perceptions. Pride leaves little room for the wisdom and insight of others. With pride, we remain interested only in information confirming what we already believe is true. It matters little whether we stake out a prideful state of superiority or inferiority; either way dulls our sensitivity to our vulnerability and diminishes our empathy for the needs of others.

> It matters little whether we stake out a prideful state of superiority or inferiority; either way dulls our sensitivity to our vulnerability and diminishes our empathy for the needs of others.

The judgmental spirit that often accompanies pride alienates us from our own true selves and from those around us. Pride also has a way of carving these flawed perceptions into stone. The more rigid our pride and judgment, the more resistant we are to healing LOVE and the transforming grace it can impart to us and through us to others. Pride, like envy and boasting, is antithetical to the trusting openness and life-giving freedom found in LOVE. Each one restricts and inhibits abundant life.

Some Healing LOVE Opposites

The familiar 1 Corinthians 13 passage also reminds that healing LOVE is relational, going to the "how" of relationships. "[Love is not] rude. It does not insist on its own way; it is not irritable or resentful" (v. 5). All of these behaviors address how we approach relationships with others and ourselves. There is a world of difference between a LOVE orientation and the approach of these healing LOVE opposites.

Generated by the insecurities of destructive fear, these latter behaviors naturally produce and reinforce a self-seeking and self-serving mindset. They go hand-in-hand with the forgetfulness about the "two things" listed in the 12-Step mantra—especially that "I am not God." When we are taking on the mantle of prideful "godhood," it is easy to claim the sense of entitlement and self-derived authority to stand in judgment of everyone and everything around us. If we are relating to others as objects, we are seeing them as mere tools for serving and gratifying our selfish needs. This naturally leads to our treating others with rudeness and disrespect.

This negative treatment of others takes many forms. We see public expressions of it in the media and political arena where judgments and discourse often demean and disparage opponents and those who are merely different from the speaker. Misrepresentation, exaggeration, and outright lying about others become permissible and acceptable once disrespect is given free rein. Open disrespect, whether public or private, does little toward building relationships or understanding. Such speech merely prompts a retaliatory disrespect that further alienates and divides.

Sometimes the disrespect is more subtle and indirect. Broad generalizations such as racism, sexism, or ageism—while not necessarily directed at a particular individual—demean and devalue whole classes of people. Prejudging and discounting people strictly because of their skin color, gender, sexual orientation, cultural background, or age diminish the wider human community, denying a wealth of potential but unrecognized contributions that could have been given or received.

Self-seeking disrespect for others can also be cleverly disguised. What appears to be honor and respect can simply be an act—a manipulation—to get something from others. Feigning respect and interest in others may merely be inducing them toward lowering their guard and extending their trust. Sellers of products and ideas may sometimes employ this form of disrespectful manipulation.

As we might expect, building trust upon falsehood and deception rarely results in a good, long-term outcome. Not only is the ill-gotten trust destroyed if the deception is discovered, but also the very act of being deceptive generates its own suspicious and distrustful worldview within the deceiver. Disrespectful deception ultimately undermines the trust of both parties and limits the potential depth of their relationship.

> Disrespectful deception ultimately undermines the trust of both parties and limits the potential depth of their relationship.

As with rudeness and disrespect, irritability and resentfulness sow destructiveness in relationships. Both flow naturally from the self-serving and self-seeking mindset. "Irritable" is translated "easily angered" in the New International Version of the Bible. Anger, in itself, is neither good nor bad. It is an internal response to a perceived external threat, providing the energy needed for taking actions to protect our own selves. Although we might often frame our anger as something caused by actions of outside forces or by what happens to us, the true source of anger lies within us and comes from those things inside us that are triggered. It is our own sensitivities bringing out the reaction of anger.

Suppose another person hugs me tightly. If I desire this hug, I experience it as an expression of love and comfort. But if the hug is uninvited and unwelcome, my response may well be anger and vigorous efforts to push the other away. The same physical action—a hug—provokes radically different reactions because of my internal interpretation of the other's action. In a similar way, my internal dialogue and interpretation drive all my feeling responses.

Irritability and angry reactions to perceived threats come easily when we are relating to others from a self-serving and self-seeking mindset. When we are the center of our own universe, we are, by our self-location, always surrounded by threat. In this self-centered mindset we have little empathy for the needs and feelings of others. We instead become hypersensitive to the threatening potential of any question, action, or slight whether threat is actually intended or not. Our heightened internal perception of threat actually produces the angry actions and reactions that result.

When we are enmeshed in this self-focused and destructive stance, we are unlikely to recognize our internal responsibility for our actions; instead, we may go in the opposite direction. Seeking to justify our actions, we are much more likely to blame other people or external circumstances. We may keep and rehash a long list of wrongs we perceive have been inflicted on us as we work on building a case for the "rightness" of our actions. When we use selective record-keeping, we avoid looking at our part in any relationally destructive interactions and gather more ammunition for justifying future anger.

> When we use selective record-keeping,
> we avoid looking at our part in any relationally destructive interactions
> and gather more ammunition for justifying future anger.

Remembering wrongs done to us in the past is not necessarily bad. Remembering may be wise when we can exercise prudent cautiousness while maintaining safe boundaries around those who have violated our trust in the past. But record-keeping becomes destructive when we use painful memories as weapons we can deploy in future retaliations. This destructive form of record-keeping allows us to preserve an unyielding self-perception that the source of problems in relationships resides outside us and within the other. Rigid, responsibility-denying, and reactive, this approach does little toward resolving differences and might very well trigger a corresponding angry and reactive response in the other. Sadly, this stance not only is reinforcing our misperception that we are the constantly threatened center of our universe, but is also setting up and perpetuating a recurring, irresolvable cycle preventing the establishment of lasting trust.

Describing LOVE
(Part 2)

The discourse in 1 Corinthians 13 on LOVE continues with this contrast: "[Love] does not rejoice in wrongdoing, but rejoices in the truth" (v.6). Wrongdoing (or "evil" in the NIV) can be difficult to define. Experience teaches us that evil is inextricably intertwined with destructive fear, eluding definition because it is synonymous with untruth—lies. The 1 Corinthians passage highlights the stark contrast between the "evil" that healing LOVE does not delight in with the "truth" with which LOVE rejoices.

While both destructive fear and evil are sustained and perpetuated by lies, evil is the end result of those lies pushed to their most destructive conclusion. Like a raging wildfire beginning from a single spark, the many lies accompanying fear eventually produce the unrestrained destructiveness of evil.

Evil is not only the culmination of the untruths supporting it, but also the logical outcome of all that is not healing LOVE—envy, boasting, pride, rudeness, self-seeking disrespect, irritability, and resentfulness. All of these are maintained and perpetuated by the lies we tell ourselves; together they will produce the fruit—evil.

There may not be a more diabolical lie than the assertion that evil is delightful. Enticing us by the immediate rush of power that often accompanies it, this seductive lie minimizes the devastating destructiveness of evil within our own selves, our relationships, and the wider world. Seeing delight in evil fuels more lies, yielding more hurtful actions.

Unlike this dysfunctional and life-robbing existence devolving out of the toxic mix of destructive fear, evil, and their lies, healing LOVE offers this simple but transforming affirmation: "[Love] rejoices with the truth." Rather than hiding from truth, or maintaining a self-view and world-view built on lies, LOVE lives and loves within the world as it is—in its weaknesses and strengths, in its joys and sorrows, and in its neediness and abundance.

> LOVE lives and loves within the world as it is—in its weaknesses and strengths, in its joys and sorrows, and in its neediness and abundance.

This is not a begrudging acceptance of truth; it comes with a joy and a trust, believing that truth brings real freedom and new opportunity. Healing LOVE is undaunted by the insecurities and uncertainties cultivated in fear, living instead and loving with a confident trust in the Giver. LOVE willingly and trustingly joins with the Giving Creator, participating in and extending the dance of giving, receiving, and giving again.

This freedom found in truth and the confident trust in the Creator provide the context for a stream of summary affirmations. "[Love] bears all things, believes all things, hopes all things, [and] endures all things" (1 Cor. 13:7). At first glance, these affirmations may appear out of touch with the realities of human living. We can easily find enumerable examples of harm, betrayal, disappointment, and failure experienced by recipients of LOVE. How can these unwanted results occur if LOVE is "bearing all things"?

The truthfulness of these affirmations becomes clearer as we recognize that these are not promises of immediate result but promises of intent. As LOVE lives and loves within the world as it is, it too is subject to limitations within creation given by the Creator. When limited security, limited resources, limited knowledge, and limited choice are combined with the ongoing coercive choices of others (and ourselves), they make a recipe that can leave the intent of LOVE unfulfilled—at least in the short term. LOVE's intended results may be continually thwarted and frustrated by all these limiting obstacles. Despite this, the intent of LOVE remains undeterred and persistent. Within the constraints of limitation, LOVE unceasingly persists in efforts toward shielding, believing in, and hoping for the best in those toward whom it is directed.

> Within the constraints of limitation, LOVE unceasingly persists in efforts toward shielding, believing in, and hoping for the best in those toward whom it is directed.

Even in the face of harmful results, betrayal, disappointment, and failure, this constant and enduring focus creates the safe and secure space that is always inviting, encouraging, and making possible trusting and giving.

Coming to recognize that the Giving Creator embodies this kind of love, we begin to get a clearer understanding of the radical distinctions between destructive fear and healing LOVE and between a god of fear and the God of LOVE. These distinctions have profound implications for relationships with ourselves, with others, and with the higher power we choose to fear, revere, and worship.

If destructive fear forms the basis for our relationships and our understanding of our world, then distrust, division, distortion, and destructiveness become the norm. When we are following the promptings of fear, our natural stance is taking from the world around us and holding what we have more tightly. Fear instills the constant concern that there will not be enough or that we will lose what we have. The common result of this worldview is a loss of connection with self, others, and the wider world. Even though the originating motivation for our actions might be a search for security, the end result is isolation, relentless insecurity, and meaninglessness—lostness.

LOVE brings something qualitatively different. If LOVE forms the basis for a relationship, then trust, unity, truthfulness, and healing constructiveness are actively at work. The persistent and enduring qualities of LOVE naturally create a zone of safety and security. Within LOVE, our relationships are built up instead of being torn apart. Relationships built within LOVE live in the trust that all that is needed will be supplied. This security allows us to hold more loosely what comes to us and freely let go to others as they have need. LOVE builds new and healing connections with our own selves, others, and the world at large.

Grace

Grace is the currency of LOVE, for it is through the giving of grace that healing LOVE is extended. We receive LOVE through receiving the gift of grace. Grace supplies the trust, unity, truthfulness, and healing constructiveness that are needed.

Grace itself is hard to pin down and transcends words we might use in defining it. Grace is not so much seen with the eyes as it is experienced through the healing and transformation it leaves behind as it passes through us. Our intuition tells us that grace is unmerited and unearned, given and not taken. Grace cannot be stored but instead flows where it is needed. We cannot demand grace, though it often responds to requests fueled by need. Whether requested or not, the flow of grace is best received with openness, gratitude, and a willingness that allow it to pass through us to others.

> The flow of grace is best received with openness, gratitude, and a willingness that allows it to pass through us to others.

Grace, this currency of healing LOVE, flows counter to all we know of destructive fear and especially in the way it relates to neediness and vulnerability. Unlike destructive fear, which dreads and avoids any semblance of vulnerability, grace welcomes, seems drawn to, and even delights in need and the prospect of meeting the need. Grace finds in need the opportunity to give and willingly flows in response to the need. When grace—this gift of LOVE—enters the picture, neediness and vulnerability are no longer liabilities. Instead, these become doorways, opening up new expressions of the dance of giving, receiving, and giving again with trust.

Within the realm where LOVE and the flow of grace have preeminence, relationships to power and the exercise of authority are dramatically altered. Weakness becomes a source of strength—vulnerability, a pathway to trust. This appears to be what the Apostle Paul discovered in 2 Corinthians 12. Constrained by an unnamed "thorn in the flesh," he earnestly prayed three times that the thorn could be removed. The response from the God of LOVE was simple: "My grace is sufficient for you, for power is made perfect in weakness" (v. 9a). This response radically shifted the way Paul framed and understood his own limitations and life challenges. He concludes, "So, I will boast all the more gladly of my weaknesses, so that the power of Christ may dwell in me. Therefore I am content with weaknesses, insults, hardships, persecutions, and calamities for the sake of Christ; for whenever I am weak, then I am strong" (vv. 9b-10).

For Paul, weakness, vulnerability, and hardship became opportunities for practicing trust and experiencing the flow of sustaining grace. With his continuing trust, Paul found new evidence of the capacity of grace to meet his need in each challenge and an ongoing invitation to extend that grace to those around him. Paul found a qualitatively different kind of strength and power as he joined in the dance of giving, receiving, and giving again with trust.

The Source behind healing LOVE and the grace that LOVE supplies is the Giving Creator God. As we recognize this, we are once again confronted with the implications of seeing the world from this life-altering viewpoint. If the Creator God focuses on giving where vulnerability and weakness abide, this response speaks volumes about the priorities and values embodied by the Creator. It offers invaluable instruction to the creation about the intended nature of relationships within the creation. If these values of the Creator are truly declaring what is most important, then these priorities are surely the wisest and most fulfilling path for the creation to follow.

> If the values of the Creator are truly declaring what is most important, then these priorities are surely the wisest and most fulfilling path for the creation to follow.

Though the simplicity and inherent logic of following the priorities of the Creator might seem obvious, the distortions of destructive fear have obscured and disputed this rationality through the past and into the present. Recognizing fears' distortions and coming to an intellectual understanding of the long-term benefits of living within the boundaries of LOVE is not the same as actually living it. But the invitation of LOVE is embedded in the gracing LOVE that is given. This LOVE that is patient, kind, and rejoices with the truth is persistent in seeking out the needy and vulnerable that are lost in the many distortions and destructions of fear. Seen from the Giving Creator's perspective, we are all included in this group of the needy and vulnerable—though we may not recognize it or admit it. All are invited to respond to this LOVE that seeks out and extends the flow of grace to all those who are lost.

A Window from Scripture

Grumbling about Grace
(Matt. 20:1-16)

Grace can seem unfair. This parable of Jesus reminds us that grace can be resisted—especially when the grace we desire is also extended to others.

> "For the kingdom of heaven is like a landowner who went out early in the morning to hire laborers for his vineyard. After agreeing with the laborers for the usual daily wage, he sent them into his vineyard. When he went out about nine o'clock, he saw others standing idle in the marketplace; and he said to them, 'You also go into the vineyard, and I will pay you whatever is right.' So they went. When he went out again about noon and about three o'clock, he did the same. And about five o'clock he went out and found others standing around; and he said to them, 'Why are you standing here idle all day?' They said to him, 'Because no one has hired us.' He said to them, 'You also go into the vineyard.' When evening came, the owner of the vineyard said to his manager, 'Call the laborers and give them their pay, beginning with the last and then going to the first.' When those hired about five o'clock came, each of them received the usual daily wage. Now when the first came, they thought they would receive more; but each of them also received the usual daily wage. And when they received it, they grumbled against the landowner, saying, 'These last worked only one hour, and you have made them equal to us who have borne the burden of the day and the scorching heat.' But he replied to one of them, 'Friend, I am doing you no wrong; did you not agree with me for the usual daily wage? Take what belongs to you and go; I choose to give to this last the same as I give to you. Am I not allowed to do what I choose with what belongs to me? Or are you envious because I am generous?' So the last will be first, and the first will be last."

"They grumbled against the landowner, saying, 'these last worked one hour, and you have made them equal to us who have borne the burden of the day and the scorching heat.'" It's easy to sympathize with these all-day workers. They showed up at dawn, put in a hard day's work during the toughest time of the day and were ready to receive the promised fruit of their labor—the usual daily wage. Nothing was amiss until the one-hour workers received the same usual daily wage promised to the all-day workers.

For the all-day workers, this initially looked like good news. If the one-hour workers got a full day's pay, fairness would dictate that the all-day workers would get even more. Working all day in the heat of the sun, they knew they deserved more. Upon receiving the same wage—the promised usual daily wage—they grumbled. It felt unfair. Grace is not fair.

This "for the kingdom of heaven is like" parable of Jesus is a parable about grace. The all-day workers were paid their due—their earned wage. This usual daily wage provided food for the belly, clothes on the back, and shelter for the night. But a need for these basic necessities persisted whether workers could work all day or not. Seeing this, the landowner in his generosity gave what was needed. A spirit of generosity fueled the grace—not the worthiness of the recipients or the value of their work.

Jesus is inviting his hearers into a trusting relationship with the Giver, depending on the Giver's generosity for the meeting of needs. If we are living in a world of fear, trusting in grace is quite a leap of faith. Being self-sufficient, depending on our wits, and securing the earnings of our own labors feels safer. Grace divests us of self-pride—the illusion that our value is derived from what we do, what we earn, or what we have. With grace, we stand on equal ground, losing perceived comparative advantages over our neighbors. These triggering insecurities fuel our resistance to grace. Trusting grace is hard when fear is distorting our thinking.

While joining with the grumbling all-day workers and resisting grace is tempting, Jesus' invitation of grace still beckons. Calling us into the joy of the Giver's generosity and the celebration of needs being met through grace, Jesus encourages his hearers to open their hearts for receiving.

Will we resist grace or be receptive to grace? The choice is ours.

Responding to LOVE

How do we best respond to this invitation of LOVE and grace? With vulnerability, trust, and our own freely chosen expressions of love. Responding to LOVE in a life-giving way involves a leap of faith—a radical shift in our relationship to limitation, neediness, and vulnerability. While destructive fear would have us resist limitation and avoid vulnerability, this gracing LOVE invites us into trust and the embracing of them, inviting us to own—to perhaps even celebrate—our vulnerabilities and weaknesses.

This response is a massive leap of trust. It may seem like the height of foolishness and totally counter to the way we have been programmed to relate to the world. Wouldn't revealing our vulnerability expose us to greater harm and exploitation?

The truthfulness of LOVE would not deny this risk. LOVE trusts a different vision and paints a larger picture exposing the true costs of guardedness. Practicing guardedness might be offering protection from dreaded consequences, but LOVE reminds us that this same guardedness is also walling us off from receiving the grace found in the fullness of love. Our distrustful guardedness is thereby limiting our capacity for receiving the healing grace we need.

Knowing the full risks and benefits, the Giving Creator of LOVE invites us to respond with vulnerability and trust anyway—despite the real and imagined risks exposed by an unguarded trust. LOVE keeps calling for a leap of faith that would transform life and living. Can we trust that openness to LOVE and responding with love outweigh all the risks of trusting? Can we believe that this gracing LOVE promises security extending even beyond the grave? Making this leap and responding to LOVE is up to us: LOVE does not and will not coerce or demand our response.

> LOVE keeps calling for a leap of faith that would transform life and living.
> Making this leap and responding to LOVE is up to us:
> LOVE does not and will not coerce or demand our response.

We might hope to be ones who would immediately respond to LOVE with genuine trust, but oftentimes it is a quiet desperation sparking the affirmative response to LOVE. In these cases, a begrudging but desperate recognition of vulnerability activates the grace, and trust follows. Something similar to this seems to have happened to the younger son in Jesus' "Parable of the Two Lost Sons."

Knowing how the story ends, we may forget that this son made the choice to return with little hope for anything akin to the grace-filled reception he would receive. His choice to return, at least at the time he made it, was just an act of desperation. The very best possibility he could imagine was being received back as a hired servant—nothing more. He surely did not expect the flow of grace he would actually experience. The telling of his story ends with the grace-filled celebration, but there can be little doubt the ending of the story was just the beginning of an ongoing story of grace. This once lost son, found by grace, could now live in the grace-inspired trust he found embodied in the healing LOVE of the father—the One who was and is the Giving Creator of LOVE.

The Apostle Paul's experience is equally instructive. He too was desperate. The oppression of his unnamed "thorn in the flesh" was overpowering. But unlike the younger son in the parable, he at least knew he could bring his concerns to the God of healing LOVE. His previous experiences with grace had already transformed him from a narrow, bigoted, murder-complicit, persecutor of Christians to a missionary advocating a gospel of LOVE for all. Even so, the vulnerability exposed in his "thorn in the flesh" introduced him to a different dimension of grace. This vulnerability-induced grace generated a trust capable of sustaining him in any circumstance or challenge.

The sustaining quality of trust that Paul found is more than some abstract, intellectual concept. This trust was and is lived out in concrete choices, exercising trust-filled *submitting love*. Once Paul discerned the message that "my grace is sufficient for you," he no longer had a need to have the "thorn" removed. He was obedient to the Giver of the message and trusted that the promised grace would indeed be sufficient. If the God of LOVE were asking Paul to live with his "thorn," he would willingly obey with trust. His submissive obedience sprang directly from his implicit trust in the Giver of LOVE and his confident assurance in the faithfulness of the promise.

> Paul's submissive obedience sprang directly from his implicit trust in the Giver of LOVE and his confident assurance in the faithfulness of the promise.

There is an unfathomable difference between this healing and *trust-filled obedience* to the Giver of gracing LOVE and the more familiar, compliant, and coerced "obedience" that we might be expected to render to the humanly imaged god of fear we previously described. Unlike the sheer terror, shame, guilt, and distrustful insecurity evoked by that destructive fear-derived deity, the relationship to the Giver of LOVE brings acceptance, forgiveness, and a peace "which surpasses all understanding" (Phil. 4:7a).

Within the context of trust-filled submitting love, the interpretation of biblical phrases such as "Fear God," "Fear the LORD," and "Fear of the LORD" is no longer about "terror and dread." Safely within the healing LOVE of the Creator, this "fear" is transformed into "trust-filled awe and wonder." The motivation for obedience no longer needs to be about avoiding the fearful anticipated consequences of disobedience. Instead, this trust-filled submitting love is a free and willing response of trust, offering a readiness to receive this grace-filled transformation and the sustaining security it provides. This is the "fear of God" that truly transforms destructive fear.

This healing response of trust-filled obedience found in submitting love is closely allied with the *transparent honesty* of *revealing love*. We have already noted that LOVE "rejoices in the truth." A trusting response to LOVE includes a willingness to be open and honest about our real selves—both with others and with our own selves. The transparent honesty of revealing love is most evident as we openly acknowledge our neediness and vulnerability.

We see a form of this in the honest self-appraisal of the younger "lost" son when he said to his father, "Father, I have sinned against heaven and before you; I am no longer worthy to be called your son" (Luke 15:21). These words were the culmination of the honest self-conversation beginning when the young man found himself at his lowest point and recognized the truth of his neediness and vulnerability. His selfdeifying choices may have placed him in those depths, but now with genuine, honest humility he acknowledged his vulnerability and became ready to receive healing grace.

Even still, his transparent honesty came more from the pressures of desperation rather than a self-chosen, willing step of trust. In a similar way, we may also have times when we are exercising the honest choice simply because we have exhausted all other avenues of protecting vulnerability. LOVE invites us to something even better: a more genuine, heartfelt trust. This trust would embrace our own vulnerability with transparent honesty first—even when less honest choices are still available. Our response of revealing love proactively relies on trust-filled faith in the sufficiency of the grace of the Giving Creator and the "power made perfect in weakness." As we follow this trust, our response becomes a freely chosen, proactive way of relating to the world. Revealing love does not deny the real risks coming with exposure to our vulnerability. It relies instead on the safety net of LOVE and the constant flow of renewing grace.

> Revealing love does not deny the real risks coming with exposure to our vulnerability. It relies instead on the safety net of LOVE and the constant flow of renewing grace.

Vulnerability and trust are also revealed in a third healing response to love—grateful, *giving love*. As we have been reminded again and again, giving is a fundamental characteristic of the Creator. The Creator of LOVE initiates the dance of giving and invites us to join in. Within the dance, gratitude becomes a natural response as we recognize that all we have and all we are is a gift.

When we mistakenly see the gifts we have received as our entitlement or falsely believe we have earned or deserved them, we tend to hold them more tightly and defensively guard them from the world. Seeing them as the gift they truly are brings gratitude and a willingness to share what we have received with others. Gratitude and sharing thus become another way of expressing trust in the Giving Creator. This trust allows us to let go of what we have received, giving it away even when it makes us seemingly more vulnerable, trusting we will be given what we need at the proper time.

Like trust-filled obedience and transparent honesty, *grateful giving* is a proactive choice, responding to the gracing LOVE we have both received and confidently trust will continue flowing from the Giving Creator. With this response we are choosing to accept the invitation to the dance of giving, receiving, and giving again with trust. Grateful for what we have received for our need, we can freely give of what we have received to meet the needs of the wider world.

> Grateful for what we have received for our need, we can freely give of what we have received to meet the needs of the wider world.

Grateful giving love flows naturally into a fourth healing response to LOVE: the rendering of sacrificial *serving love*. Unlike fear-inspired service that has its origins in and focuses on meeting our own selfish needs, sacrificial serving love looks to meeting the needs of others. Philippians 2:3-4 articulates this attitude: "Do nothing from selfish ambition or conceit, but in humility regard others as better than yourselves. Let each of you look not to your own interests, but to the interests of others." This response to LOVE mirrors the action of the Giving Creator.

Like the other three responses to LOVE, sacrificial serving love involves and incorporates vulnerability and trust. This fourth response also utilizes an additional dimension: the recognition that our vulnerabilities are resources that can be used in the service of others. While once viewed as liabilities, our vulnerabilities can be trusted to give compassionate insight into identifying and meeting the needs of others. With this understanding, those of us who face or have faced health challenges can more sensitively assist those currently having them. In like fashion, those who have formerly been victimized by abuse can reach out to those now being victimized. As 12-Step recovery groups demonstrate, addicts are often helped best by other recovering addicts who have awareness and ownership of their own addictions.

Sacrificial serving love—owning our vulnerabilities for the purpose of serving others—lives out the dance of giving, receiving, and giving again with trust. All of us are needy and need others. Through serving love we together meet the needs of one another and the lives of all of us are thereby enriched. When we do as LOVE would teach us and give our new "riches" away, together we are further enriched. This dance of love, trust, and abundant, ever-giving life is the original and ongoing intention of the Giving Creator of LOVE.

These four healing and proactive responses to LOVE—trust-filled obedience, transparent honesty, grateful giving, and sacrificial service—all support and reinforce each other, creating the conditions where nurture, security, and all the qualities of LOVE can fully blossom. In a sense, our choosing these four responses and the attitudes and behaviors accompanying them free us to be co-creators with the Creator God of LOVE.

These responses that trustingly embrace the Creator's gracing LOVE not only fulfill the Giving Creator's vision for humanity to be "made in the image of God," but they also transform and disarm destructive fear. Within the safe zone created by LOVE and these responses to LOVE, destructive fear and its effects are transformed and healed.

Despite all this, the decision about embracing LOVE and exercising these healing responses remains with us. In each moment, we have the freedom to choose (and to re-choose) LOVE and these life-giving responses of love. Each moment we exercise this healing proactive choice, we are supplied with the grace needed to carry us to the next moment. In that next moment, a new choice for practicing love presents itself for our decision. And so it goes. While proactive responses to LOVE may still carry risks for the one responding, the choice of embracing and exercising love is always available.

> While proactive responses to LOVE may still carry risks for the one responding, the choice of embracing and exercising love is always available.

At the same time, we always have the freedom of not choosing LOVE or not choosing at all (which is also a choice.) Both of these latter choices insert us back into the clutches of destructive fear. But whether we exercised the better choice with our last choice or not, this capacity for choice-making remains an ongoing gift from the Creator of LOVE. With each moment we always have a new opportunity for embracing a response of love. No matter how far away we have traveled in our lostness in destructive fear, we can always choose the healing and proactive responses to love and again be found by grace and LOVE. The younger son's story in Jesus' parable can always be our story.

Unfortunately, the older son's story can also be our story. Because of his resistance to grace and LOVE, he remained lost at the end of Jesus' telling of the story. By his own choice, he remained outside and alienated from relationship with his brother, the Giving Father, and all who would join the celebration of grace. Despite the destructiveness and alienation of this older son's choice, the Giving Father did not force him to join the party of grace. A healing response to LOVE is always a free choice—never a coerced or demanded choice. Though the story ends with the older son remaining outside, the vision of grace and LOVE this parable presents clearly teaches that the welcome of grace is available to him the moment he chooses to receive it. With every moment, each of us has the opportunity to respond to the invitation of the Giving Creator of LOVE and choose healing, proactive responses of love.

> With every moment, each of us has the opportunity to respond to the invitation of the Giving Creator of LOVE and choose healing, proactive responses of love.

In the next four chapters, we will look more closely at these four love responses: submitting, revealing, giving, and serving and the ways they are expressed through trust-filled obedience, transparent honesty, grateful giving, and sacrificial service. Each of them is accompanied by attitudes and behaviors that not only reflect LOVE but also counter, disarm, and transform the earlier described destructive, distortive, and depersonalizing attitudes and behaviors produced by destructive fear. Hopefully, a clearer understanding of the practical application of proactively choosing love responses will assist us in actually living them out.

Questions for Reflection

1. How have images of a God of fear impacted your faith journey, and how might an understanding of a God of LOVE change your faith perspective? How does this difference reframe your motivation for pursuing faith?
2. How has envy or boasting or pride hindered your relationships or the relationships of others you have known? What changes within you when you begin taking responsibility for your contribution to conflict? How might this invoke changes in others?
3. How might the affirmation that "Love rejoices with the truth" give you strength when you are facing unwanted realities? How might a belief in this encourage you toward reaching outside yourself for help?
4. What fears prevent you from owning the sources of your vulnerability? When is it easier to trust? When is it harder?
5. How have difficult experiences in your life equipped you to offer better assistance to others going through challenges?

A Window from Scripture

The Philippian Hymn
(Phil. 2:5-11)

Christian faith asserts, "Jesus Christ is Lord." This "Philippian Hymn" gives a paradigm-shifting understanding of "lordship."

> Let the same mind be in you that was in Christ Jesus, who, though he was in the form of God, did not regard equality with God as something to be exploited, but emptied himself, taking the form of a slave, being born in human likeness. And being found in human form, he humbled himself and became obedient to the point of death—even death on a cross. Therefore God also highly exalted him and gave him the name that

> is above every name, so that at the name of Jesus every knee should bend, in heaven and on earth and under the earth, and every tongue should confess that Jesus Christ is Lord, to the glory of God the Father.

In this hymn, the "lordship" Jesus embodies is empowered by healing LOVE. Jesus' "lordship" is not derived from the power to coerce and terrify subjects with the threat of suffering, but is given in response to his modeled trust, humility, and willingness to be the sufferer. This radical shift away from grasping control and toward obedient submissiveness defies all that we know and experience. Jesus' "lordship" represents a refusal of the trappings of coercive, dominating power and instead embraces servanthood and vulnerability. If this example of Jesus were the lens we use for viewing the Creator God, would it not transform our understanding of God and the values the Creator God endorses?

If Jesus is Lord and Jesus is God—as Christian faith affirms—then the trusting, self-denying, and self-giving actions and choices of Jesus would logically reflect the most important values within the Godhead. Any doubts about this assertion would be dispelled when, in this hymn, Jesus is exalted to the highest place because he exercised trust, humility, and obedience all the way through death. If we are to believe these words, then they present a God characterized by self-giving love and the willingness to suffer with and for the creation.

How might this radical shift in our understanding of the character and values of God transform our relationships with God, with others, and with ourselves? For starters, this understanding makes possible new levels of trust in each of these relationships. "Every knee should bow" and "every tongue confess" would not be coerced reactions of holy terror but would be transformed into freely given, heartfelt responses of loving trust. Relationships with others could be transformed from being self-serving and suspicious to being collaborative, trusting, and mutually supportive. Our relationships with our own selves could be transformed from the obsessiveness to avoid vulnerability to a trust-filled willingness to embrace it. What might happen if this paradigm-shifting understanding were actually believed, trusted, and lived out by faith?

Chapter 7
Transforming Controlling Fear with Submitting Love

Trusting Submissiveness

Being human is an amazing gift! Envisioning a loving and giving Creator God behind this gift qualitatively changes how we see ourselves and how we see the world around us. It prompts us to recognize the grace that constantly surrounds us, receive its healing flow, and allow this grace to pass through us to others. Visualizing a loving Creator God focused on giving naturally sets in motion a dance of giving, receiving, and giving again with trust. We are invited to join in the dance.

Would our envisioning a loving Creator God require this Giver also to be vulnerable? Not necessarily. Could we not imagine a creator god who is giving and loving on many levels but still maintains a protected distance from the creation? Could we not imagine a giving and loving god retaining the power to compel obedience if and when the human creation chose to decline the invitation to dance?

Maybe so, but this would not be the God revealed in the words of the Philippian hymn (Phil. 2:5-11). The God revealed in Jesus and by Jesus willingly embraces vulnerability all the way through death. In Jesus, Godhood repudiates coercive power and demonstrates a wholehearted trust in the healing power of vulnerable LOVE. There remains no place for domination, grasping, deception, or control and the destructive fear generating and sustaining them. The vulnerable, healing LOVE found within this Creator God and embodied in Jesus drives out destructive fear.

Words cannot explain the why and the how of this self-giving, trust-filled obedience of Jesus and his submissive willingness to embrace suffering. But his actions personalize our understanding of this loving and giving Creator God. No longer just an abstract and distant concept we only carry in our minds, the God revealed in Jesus embraces the very real pain, vulnerability, and limitedness characterizing the human condition.

> The God revealed in Jesus embraces the very real pain, vulnerability, and limitedness characterizing the human condition.

Perhaps even more personally important, this loving, giving, and yet personal Creator God knows, experiences, and embraces the very real pain, vulnerability, and limitedness that we each experience in our individual lives. As we take seriously this vulnerable and giving Creator God embodied in Jesus, we find the only God truly worthy of both our worship and our trust. Trusting this understanding also releases us from a common theological dilemma.

Those who try to integrate a god they describe as "loving" with a god still using all the dominating and grasping tools of fear for maintaining control face an insurmountable challenge. While this commonly understood—but internally inconsistent—god might still evoke a fear-based compliance, how could it invite genuine trust and love? In contrast, we find the very embodiment of healing LOVE with this vulnerable and giving Creator God, revealed and embodied in Jesus. This God is extending a personal invitation to a freely chosen, trust-filled, and submissive obedience. If we respond with submitting love, the fruit of LOVE—grace—is naturally made available, passing through us, assisting wherever there are needs.

Receiving the invitation does not automatically activate our choice to trust. This is an invitation to trust—not a demand. How do we initiate this movement toward trust-filled submissiveness? How do we let go of our fears, our resistance, and our experience-based distrustfulness so we can exercise the required trust? How do we progress from wanting to make the leap of faith to actually making it?

As a starting point, we cannot get around the reality that even trust itself is a gift of grace. No matter how much trust we might muster on our own, an honest appraisal would still leave us with the recognition that we have an inadequate level of trust. Like the desperate father who brought his ill son to Jesus in Mark 9:24, we at best can only say, "I believe, help my unbelief!" We find in this gospel story that it was the father's vulnerable admission of need that unleashed the healing flow of grace for his son. In our own stories, our admission of need can be the catalyst allowing the grace of trust to flow to us and through us.

Experience teaches that admitting our own neediness is most difficult if we are the first one in the group making that vulnerable admission. Jesus' example reminds us that we are not the ones going first. As fully human and yet as God, Jesus lived out his own trusting and submissive obedience in the Garden of Gethsemane the night before he died on the cross.

Here, interacting with the Giving Creator God he knew intimately as "Abba (Father)," he laid out both his concerns and his ultimate trust. Matthew's gospel records two prayers sandwiched around a plea to his disciples for needed support. The first time Jesus prayed, "My Father, if it is possible, let this cup [the suffering prior to and during his death on the cross] pass from me; yet not what I want but what you want" (26:39). After recognizing and acknowledging the sleepy disciples' limited support in that moment, Jesus prayed a second time, "My Father, if this cannot pass unless I drink it, your will be done" (v. 42).

We can see the exercise of Jesus' trust-filled, submitting love as he prayed "not what I want but what you want" and "your will be done." This exercising is not

Transforming Controlling Fear with Submitting Love

some naïve and blind obedience denying the obstacles and the gravity this obedience requires. Jesus was fully aware of his vulnerability and the personal cost he would endure. Nevertheless, he trustingly chose submission to the Father's will. He trusted his obedient actions would express vulnerable love, supplying needed and transformative grace throughout the whole of creation, flowing forth and planting the seeds of LOVE in places once occupied by destructive fear. When Jesus obeyed all the way through death, he demonstrated and unleashed a healing flow of gracing LOVE that could penetrate anywhere and transform fear everywhere.

This abundant supply of LOVE is sorely needed if we also are choosing this path of trust-filled, submitting love. Following Jesus on this path is costly and demanding. Like Jesus, we have to stop and count the cost. The words of Jesus make this clear. "If any want to become my followers, let them deny themselves and take up their cross and follow me" (Matt. 16:24). In another place Jesus tells his disciples, "Whoever loves father or mother more than me is not worthy of me; and whoever loves son or daughter more than me is not worthy of me; and whoever does not take up the cross and follow me is not worthy of me. Those who find their life will lose it, and those who lose their life for my sake will find it" (Matt. 10:37-39).

The teachings of Jesus in the Sermon on the Mount include commands about loving enemies, praying for persecutors, going the second mile, and choosing not to resist those who would take advantage of us (see Matt. 5:38-44). In other words, Jesus' teachings encourage us to choose actions that might even broaden our vulnerability to being exploited or harmed. Jesus' words contain demands that seem impossible to fulfill, but also come with the paradoxical promise that we will find our truest selves in our exercising trust-filled and submissive obedience to the giving Creator God of LOVE. Once again, we come back to this ongoing invitation to trust: Can we, and will we, choose that first step of trust?

> Can we, and will we, choose the first step of trust?

The first step of trust is and always will be a leap of faith, but the flow of grace is constantly available, assisting us the moment we choose to leap. Seeing the trust-filled path of submitting love Jesus modeled, we recognize our own need and ready ourselves for receiving. This flow of gracing LOVE embodied in Jesus gives us what we need in that moment. Then, as we step out in trust, we are given what we need for the next moment. Just as the headlights on our car provide needed light only far enough to see the road ahead for the next few moments of our journey, so grace gives us what we need to make the next step of trust. The promise contained in living out this ongoing trust is expressed in the words of Proverbs 3:5-6: "Trust in the Lord [the Giver of LOVE] with all your heart, and do not rely on your own insight. In all your ways acknowledge him, and he will make straight your paths."

The Fruit of Submitting Love

If we choose to make this leap of trusting and submissive obedience, we find that our grace-assisted first step of faith sets us on a new and different path. Along this path, the flow of grace makes possible new attitudes and behaviors that are continually nourishing love in us and multiplying this grace all around us. Not only are these gifts of LOVE freeing and life giving, but they also offer the incalculable gift of undermining, disarming, and transforming the effects of destructive fear.

These gifts are not the product of our own efforts; they just seem to follow naturally when our choice of trusting and submissive obedience opens the gates and allows the multifaceted fruit of grace to flow to us and through us. With submitting love, the only will we are exercising is the willing choice of submitting and offering our obedience to the Giver of LOVE. This choice and all the fruit that follows are grace-filled gifts of LOVE. The words of the letter to the Ephesians describe this healing movement: "For by grace you have been saved through faith, and this is not your own doing; it is the gift of God—not the result of works, so that no one can boast" (Eph. 2:8-9).

The contrast between the trust-filled path of grace and the path of destructive fear is striking. A person on the path of fear attempts to project confidence and security to the outer world even as they are hiding and covering up a core of profound insecurity. When we are on the path of grace, we have an available source of inner security (an expectant confidence in the LOVE of the Giver of grace) sustaining us even though outward circumstances may be filled with vulnerability and risk. On the path of trust-filled obedience, we live with an ongoing expectation that the Giver of LOVE is present with us through all circumstances, helping us in our need.

> On the path of trust-filled obedience, we live with an ongoing expectation that the Giver of LOVE is present with us through all circumstances, helping us in our need.

As a chaplain, I have had occasion to observe this kind of trust modeled by patients and their families facing life-limiting conditions or imminent death. While they still might look to the Divine as a source of help through a "miracle" or lengthening of life, theirs is not just a desperate search for anything that might be able to change their unwanted situation. Instead, these individuals express a genuine trust in the loving presence of the Divine in the midst of their circumstances. As they pursue the best of medical interventions, they trust the Divine presence will give them what they truly need—whether that is longer physical life or the comfort and sustaining presence needed as we "walk through the darkest valley" (see Ps. 23:4). They often relate: "God has helped me get through tough times in the past, and I know God will be with us through this; I trust and submit myself to God's will and purpose for my life." When we can embody this quality of trust, we always have hope.

Such is not the case along the path of destructive fear. On this path an ever-present distrust shapes our expectations and gives us little reason to count on outside assistance. Looking to a god of fear does not provide a lasting source of trust. Indeed, the dominating, grasping, lying, and controlling actions characterizing this god only seem to magnify any distrust we already had. Given this distrust, might we not actually feel more secure if we just assume this god is absent or stop believing in a god at all?

This fear-filled path cultivates a distrust undermining any expectation we might have of receiving support from others. Would it not urge us to presume that they too would eventually betray us or let us down? The path of destructive fear takes us away from hope and moves us toward despair.

> The path of destructive fear takes us away from hope and moves us toward despair.

The widening gap between the trusting path of submitting love and the path of destructive fear can also be seen in our relationship with limitation. Flowing out of submissive obedience is a natural acceptance of the real limits given to us as human beings. When we rely on the gracing LOVE offered by the Giving Creator, we have no need for resisting limits or constantly searching for ways around them. Instead, with our exercising of submitting love, we trust that limited security, limited resources, limited knowledge, and limited choice are gifts of LOVE contributing toward a larger purpose. When looking through this trusting lens, we see beyond the immediate challenges brought by these limits. We recognize that these boundaries themselves make possible the freedom and joy found in the Giving Creator's intended dance of giving, receiving, and giving again. Trusting these limits allows us to join the dance.

This acceptance of human limitation also frees us from the burdens that come from trying to bend reality to our liking or to be our own god. As we found in earlier chapters, destructive fear originates through our efforts that focus on actively or passively steering our imagination toward circumventing real limits. With submitting love, we are acknowledging the truth of the "two things about God" and remembering there is a God and that we are not God ourselves. The grace-filled practice of submitting love disarms the controlling expressions of destructive fear at their source, removing the fuel that drives them.

Hope in the Giving Creator's presence and acceptance of real limits naturally bears the fruit of a genuine humility. Unlike a counterfeit humility that might be generated by our willful efforts at suppressing appearances of pride, this genuine humility comes as a natural gift of LOVE. Self-effacing comments and humble-sounding denials of our gifts might appear to demonstrate humility, but these phony forms of humility are just the flip side of pride, reflecting efforts that are more about enhancing our "specialness" in relation to others. When we begin taking pride in our "humility," we may also be revealing our darker motives.

Genuine humility allows us to accept ourselves as we are, celebrating the gifts and opportunities of each moment while being ever mindful of the Giver delighting in our being and specialness. Recognizing and trusting that the Giver's ongoing giving is the true source of our specialness, we have no need to be "more special" than anyone else. We are free to acknowledge the gifts we have received, point to the Giver who has given to us, and pass on this open and giving spirit to everyone around us. If we have authentic humility, we may be truly surprised when others notice, drawing attention to its presence.

> If we have authentic humility, we may be truly surprised when others notice, drawing attention to its presence.

Closely allied with genuine humility is a willingness to admit our need and ask for help. This runs counter to the fiercely independent, self-contained, and self-sufficient stance prized by many people in our society. Finding its origins in a fear-based perception, this mindset sees any lack in me as a diminishment in my value. A reluctance to acknowledge neediness or vulnerability will lead us to avoid them. These self-deceptive and avoidant efforts just cultivate more fear and perpetuate this destructive cycle in all its dominating, grasping, lying, and controlling expressions.

The exercise of submitting love aligns our practice with the realities of human limitation, encouraging the mutual sharing of needs and resources undergirding the dance of giving, receiving, and giving again with trust. We are limited, vulnerable, and needy beings. We need the grace of submitting love and the freedom it gives if we are to allow others to help us or if we are to find the strength to reach out to others in their need. A trust-filled practice of submitting love shapes our perspective and expands our constructive options. Not only are we freed from the judgments harshly criticizing our shortcomings or those in others, but we also discover the creative pattern of ongoing grace, disarming the anxieties generating fear while building bridges and opening new opportunities for safer relationships.

Letting Be

As we have found, the anxieties generating destructive fear and generated by fear are often expressed in controlling actions and attitudes. The end product of all these

Transforming Controlling Fear with Submitting Love

strategies of assertive control was and is a seemingly never-ending treadmill leading to emptiness, insecurity, and further fear. Experience teaches a principle of diminishing returns: the more vigorously we try to control, the less control we actually have.

Submitting love, informed by the common wisdom of this principle, offers a different path from the treadmill of fruitlessly pursuing control. With submitting love, we let go, let God, and let be. We give up the need for controlling. Through this paradoxical practice, we loosen our grip, exercise our trust, and disarm the anxiety continually fueling the fear. In letting go, letting God, and letting be, we are again living out the trusting and confident expectation that the Giver of gracing LOVE is present with us through all circumstances. Like a raindrop falling into a vast ocean, each source of anxiety can then be swallowed up in the incomprehensible vastness of the Giver's transforming LOVE. Along this healing path, our trusting choice to practice submitting love unleashes the already available grace, transforming our very being and our perception of the world around us.

The transformation made possible by this exercise of trust also broadens our options as we are considering alternatives in our decision-making. On the distrustful path of fear, this is often not the case. One of the byproducts of this destructive path is the common tendency to frame decisions or actions into "all or nothing" choices. We box ourselves into positions on the extremes. In the insecurity of distrust, our need to do "something" may bring about an impulsive reaction that proves destructive. Conversely, fears of "making a mistake" may paralyze our responsiveness and our inaction itself brings harmful effects.

> One of the byproducts of the destructive path of fear is the common tendency to frame decisions or actions in "all or nothing" choices.

The absolutism of "all or nothing" choices seldom cultivates trust in relationships but promotes adversarial conflicts and "win-lose" settlements, locking in resentments and perpetuating further conflicts. If my own distrust is keeping the other at an arm's length and I am constantly guarding against them taking advantage of my weakness, how likely am I to enter into a mutually beneficial and collaborative understanding with them? How likely is the other person to trust me if they sense my defensiveness and this triggers a feared exposure of their own vulnerabilities?

Once insecurity and distrust become the driving forces in a relationship, there is little room for the empathetic understanding each person needs of the other for discovering collaborative solutions. Without trust, each person is incentivized to take as much as they can in each interaction and give up as little as possible. Whether we are looking at relationships in international diplomacy, domestic politics, or in our closest and most intimate relationships, we find in this destructive process the perfect recipe for never-ending conflict that continually frustrates, but brings little lasting resolution. Unfortunately, the destructiveness unleashed through these dysfunctional relationships is not limited to the participants. Anyone who happens to be within the sphere of influence of these relationships can suffer collateral damage.

The practice of submitting love frees us to find a middle way, transcending the extremes and allowing a path through conflict that values the interests of each stakeholder. It promotes a "win-win" solution in the moment and lays the trusting groundwork for future collaborative endeavors. On this trusting path, we can still take action when there is a real concern our action might dangerously expose our weaknesses. Why? We remain secure within the safe arms of healing LOVE even if our weaknesses were to be exploited.

Our willingness to practice trust offers the additional benefit of allowing and encouraging the other to exercise trust. Just as distrust begets further distrust, our exercised trust invites the other to drop their guard and respond in trust. As this happens, mutual and growing trust can exponentially expand the opportunities for innovative, collaborative, and life-giving solutions for the participants. This beachhead of trust may also spread far beyond the original relationship, blessing an ever-widening circle that is touched by its influence. Exercising submitting love can potentially impact people and circumstances in ways we might never have dreamed possible.

In contrast, the path of fear generates feelings of entitlement. This happens when we misperceive our level of control within our world or we are intoxicated with a false sense of our importance. Just as with the stance of pride, an attitude of "the world owes me" likely originates with our buried insecurities about our value and worth. With the self-absorption these insecurities promote, we may use self-serving judgments, comparing ourselves to others, minimizing their contributions, and overvaluing our own. Before long, we are believing we have been short-changed and are carrying the resentful perception that we have a "right" to even the score and take what we "deserve." The more we cultivate a sense of entitlement, the more we resist the wisdom of countering views and the harder it becomes to find our way back.

The grace we discover in the exercise of submitting love provides a way back. This grace fosters genuine humility, brings recognition of the giftedness all around us, and assists us in letting go of misperceptions and misjudgments supporting a stance of entitlement. Most of all, it bestows the life-giving awareness that "I have been given much." Though this awareness that "I have been given much" could be turned into a guilt-laden demand by the distortions of destructive fear, under grace this message evokes a sense of healing gratitude, extending additional blessings to anyone around us. This realization invites our renewed expression of gratitude to the Giving Creator—joining in the dance of giving, receiving, and giving again with trust.

A final fruit of the practice of submitting love is the disarming of the fear-driven taskmaster of perfectionism. With the "anti-grace" of perfectionism, we wed together a life-sapping denial of human limitation with an imagination distorted by the insecuri-

Transforming Controlling Fear with Submitting Love

ties of fear. This striving for "perfection" sets up standards for behavior or achievement that are humanly impossible to accomplish or maintain.

> Striving for "perfection" sets up standards for behavior or achievement that are humanly impossible to accomplish or maintain.

Sometimes we may direct these perfectionistic demands upon others; sometimes we impose them on ourselves. In either case, the real source driving and empowering these coercive standards is destructive fear and fear-generated insecurities. "Do I truly have value and worth?" "Am I (and the people I care about) 'good enough'?" Perfectionism tries to answer these questions with "perfect" proof of our competence and importance. "If only I could be 'perfect,' then my value and worth could be assured." This endeavor is fruitless. Like other deceptions of destructive fear, it denies the real human limitations constraining us. Limited security, limited resources, limited knowledge, and limited choice clearly prevent the possibility of absolute perfection, frustrating and disappointing anyone who pursues it.

Pursuing absolute perfection does not pose the greatest challenge; any reasonable person would recognize its impossibility. The larger problem is holding our own selves accountable to a standard of near-perfection that still is just beyond our reach. Intellectually, we may acknowledge this goal is not possible either, but we seem to forget this when judging our achievements. Since we could almost always do more in any situation, what we actually do is never going to be quite enough—we find no endpoint or place of satisfaction. We may be telling ourselves we are just "trying to do our best"; in reality, we are placing ourselves on a treadmill of endless frustration.

> We may be telling ourselves we are just "trying to do our best"; in reality, we are placing ourselves on a treadmill of endless frustration.

If perfectionism rules, then any moments we celebrate as successful achievements are doomed to be only temporary—an accomplishment only provides a starting point for a new and higher goal. When this ever-higher goal setting gets combined with an "all or nothing" mindset, it can lock us into a self-reinforcing and perpetually miserable state of being. How can we find release from this self-imposed bondage?

Only a love-based grace can release us. The grace we find when we exercise submitting love stops the treadmill and unburdens us from this taskmaster of perfectionism. This unburdening grace utilizes all the fruits coming with the practice of submitting love; together these disarm and transform the fear-based components originating and perpetuating the striving for perfection. Expecting the Giving Creator's presence, accepting human limitation, and the expressing of genuine humility's willingness to receive help all work together to lay the groundwork. When these are combined with grace-empowered choices to let go, let God, and let be, we are given a grace-inspired awareness of the giftedness of our own life and the giftedness of all those around us.

In this grace-filled process, we discover anew that our value/worth is derived from the Giving Creator of LOVE and is no longer dependent upon what we do or fail to do. This lifts the weight of perfectionistic demands from off our shoulders, alleviating any concerns we may harbor about our deficiencies or shortcomings. These worries shrink in the comparative vastness of the reservoir of healing LOVE that the Giver of LOVE supplies.

The reminder that the Source of all we are is the giving Creator God of LOVE brings us back to where we began this chapter. Building upon the Philippian hymn, we have seen the example of Jesus who first embarked on this pathway of submitting love. His embodiment of the vulnerable, giving Creator God and his trust-filled leadership invite us toward exercising our trust, following in trust, and discovering for ourselves the healing, transformation, and fruitfulness that this Giver of LOVE makes available. We find in the grace-inspired practice of submitting love all we need to disarm and transform the controlling expressions of destructive fear. The fruit of this trust-filled submissiveness to the Giver of LOVE also grows our capacity for another healing response of trust: the transparent honesty of revealing love.

Questions for Reflection

1. How would believing in a God who "knows, experiences, and embraces the very real pain, vulnerability, and limitedness we each experience" change the way you see the world, your loved ones, and yourself? How might this belief reframe the things you do and why you do them?
2. What inhibits your personal capacity to trust? What experiences of grace help you move beyond these into greater steps of trust?
3. Share an experience where "letting go" or "letting be" changed the dynamics of a situation, opening up new possibilities for positive collaboration. What did you learn about yourself and the other party through this exchange?
4. How has a spirit of perfectionism contributed to your life in positive ways? How has it negatively impacted your life?

A Window from Scripture

A Psalm of Confession
(Ps. 51:1-10)

Wisdom teaches, "Confession is good for the soul." We find a personalized model for confession in these selected verses from Psalm 51.

> Have mercy on me, O God, according to your steadfast love; according to your abundant mercy blot out my transgressions. Wash me thoroughly from my iniquity, and cleanse me from my sin.
> For I know my transgressions, and my sin is ever before me. Against you, you alone, have I sinned, and done what is evil in your sight, so that you are justified in your sentence and blameless when you pass judgment. Indeed, I was born guilty, a sinner when my mother conceived me.
> You desire truth in the inward being; therefore teach me wisdom in my secret heart. Purge me with hyssop, and I shall be clean; wash me, and I shall be whiter than snow. Let me hear joy and gladness; let the bones that you have crushed rejoice. Hide your face from my sins, and blot out all my iniquities.
> Create in me a clean heart, O God, and put a new and right spirit within me.

Tradition associates these confessing words with David, the king who elsewhere in scripture is referred to as a man after God's own heart (see Acts 13:22). This same David had exploited his kingly authority, committed adultery with the wife of one of his soldiers off at war, and then had this husband murdered in battle, deflecting attention and covering up the pregnancy resulting from the infidelity. After an appropriate time of "mourning," the grieving widow was brought into David's home, became his wife, and bore him a son. Initially, no untoward consequences seemed evident, but 2 Samuel 11 concludes with these ominous words: "But the thing that David had done displeased the LORD."

In 2 Samuel 12, the prophet Nathan comes to David and tells a story of a gross exploitation and abuse of power inflicted upon a poor neighbor by a rich man. As David hears the story, he is enraged, condemns this rich man in the harshest terms, and demands quadruple damages be paid in restitution. David's words of righteous judgment are turned on himself when Nathan pronounces, "You are the man!"(v. 7). Confronted with the enormity of what he has done, David can only reply, "I have sinned against the LORD" (v. 13). According to tradition, the words of Psalm 51 come out of this moment of self-clarity and recognition.

Whatever the source of these words, they reflect the heartfelt remorse and genuine sense of personal responsibility that always seem to accompany truly transformative confessions. This is not the manipulative confession of one whose real regret is getting caught; this confession comes from one who is facing and feeling the enormous weight of responsibility for his hurtful actions. A genuine confession looks inward, exposing all we have done to the full light of day and yet allowing the full comprehension that our darkest selves may harbor the potential for even greater acts of destructiveness and harm. A true confession also looks outward, recognizing that our actions not only touch the immediate recipients harmed in the moment, but also are carrying consequences extending outward as the ever-widening ripples in a pond. A transformative confession enables us to see, as this psalmist suggests, that all sin—whatever its intended target—is still, at its core, sin against the Creator and a violation of the purpose for which we have being. Genuine confession dispels any pretense we might maintain about our self-righteousness.

Despite the unfathomable, destructive consequences we might discover while making this honest assessment, the words of the psalmist reflect an inherent trust in the willing capacity of the Creator God to intervene with gracing forgiveness, washing, cleansing, and restoring us to the joy of new beginning. Empowered itself by divine grace, our free exercise of heartfelt confession invites and allows the Creator to recreate the pure hearts and steadfast spirits within us that we need going forward. Although this transformative confessing may not erase the consequences of what we have done (King David's later experiences would bear this out), it does enlarge our capacity for trustworthiness in future encounters. When we realize healing forgiveness, it fosters the humility, sensitivity, and empathy that free us to be more trustworthy partners in the dance of giving, receiving, and giving again. Are we willing to take the leap of faith, expose our true selves to the light of healing LOVE, and allow the grace of experienced mercy and realized forgiveness to transform our life and living?

Chapter 8
Transforming Lying Fear with Revealing Love

Trusting Grace

Being human is an amazing gift! Trust equips us for exploring the many facets of this gift, and this same trust also sows the seeds for deeper relationships with one another. Inspired, empowered, and sustained by LOVE, this trust is an intentional, exercised choice, expressing a willingness to be vulnerable.

There is much to discourage us and dissuade us from exercising a vulnerable trust. Not only are we bombarded by our own insecurities generating the many expressions of destructive fear, but a stance of vulnerability also sets us up to be targets for the dominating, grasping, lying, and controlling actions of others. It is easier to distrust trust and slip back into the more familiar patterns of fear. How do we keep ourselves on the intentional path of trust? How do we get back on the path when we have either chosen fear responses themselves or have neglected to make any choice at all, thereby drifting back into destructive fear?

The first step of trust is and always will be a grace-empowered leap of faith. This is the case whether we are talking about our first step of trust or we are stepping back onto the path of trust after spending some or many steps along the path of fear. This choice to trust, by its very nature, cannot be a "once for always" decision. It is a series of ongoing decisions we make one at a time.

At any grace-assisted moment we have the freedom to choose trust for the next moment. We also have the freedom at any moment to turn a deaf ear to grace, stop choosing trust, and go back into the clutches of destructive fear. Though this choice-making capacity remains with us, the Giving Creator of LOVE stands ready, supplying the grace we need to make the next choice to trust. Jesus' parable portraying the loving father reminds us that grace is always focused on the current and future steps we are making—not hung up on our missteps of the past. Even when our last step was a distrustful step on the path of fear, the Giving Creator still makes possible the next step of willing trust. With the healing power of this gracing LOVE assisting us, we are always within one step of getting back on the path of trust.

> With the healing power of gracing LOVE assisting us,
> we are always within one step of getting back on the path of trust.

Recognizing that LOVE is always available to pick us back up is comforting, but the frequency of our need for this grace is troubling. Time after time and despite our best intentions, the pressures and easily available short-term benefits of reasserting our control tempt us into giving in, drifting back into the many expressions of destructive fear. How many times can we mess up, recognize we have fallen short, and ask for grace to pick us back up again? Is there a limit? Can we mess up so bad or so often that we move beyond the power of LOVE to restore us? LOVE answers, "No," and continually speaks words of boundless grace. Destructive fear has a different answer. If we are listening to fear, we may put our own limits on grace.

Limiting Grace

Destructive fear fosters a self-absorbed perspective, portraying grace as a "get out of jail free" card shielding us from the unpleasant consequences of damaging choices and providing a license to continue our present course. Initially, this "cheap grace" notion has many attractive qualities. Who would not want to take advantage of this enabling "gift," have the slate wiped clean, and be let off the hook? In the short-term, this self-absorbed, fear-derived, and exploitive response to grace seems quite appealing; it also limits our capacity to receive its benefits.

Just as the same heat of the sun softens butter and hardens brick, so our motivations and the focus of our responses to grace influence what it is able to do in us. LOVE softens the heart of those responding with a step forward on the path of trust. It hardens the heart of those who seek to use grace as a "get out of jail free" card without the corresponding step toward trust and healing.

Over time, those with softening hearts grow in their capacity for seeing, experiencing, and trusting this gracing LOVE. Those with hardening hearts regressively have a more difficult time seeing and experiencing the still boundless healing grace that is always available. A hardened heart not only harbors and cultivates destructive fear, but it also misunderstands the purposeful and trustworthy intentions of LOVE. Relying on this misunderstanding, a fear-harboring heart will distrust even when encountering trustworthiness, projecting its untrustworthiness onto everything and everyone around it.

This hardening stance of distrustfulness produces more resistance to grace. A fear-infused heart is particularly sensitive to the perceived sense of unfairness accompanying the extending of grace toward others: "Shouldn't they get what they deserve?"

LOVE would again answer, "No." Focusing more on mercy, LOVE does not play favorites but would extend the same gifting to all. This "unfair" mercy presents its own dilemma for those who might be recipients. We cannot criticize the fairness of other undeserving persons receiving healing grace without undermining any claim we might have to receiving it ourselves. Would we prefer seeing underserved grace extended to everyone, including ourselves, or the equally "fair" solution of withholding grace from everyone? Experience teaches that a hardened, fear-infused heart would rather choose the latter option: denying grace to everyone, including itself, preferring this to the transformation and healing and new beginning that a wider gracing might bring.

A self-absorbed and hardening heart refuses to see the bigger picture and larger intention behind the Giving Creator's gift of grace. Continuing to see and work from a fear-oriented perspective, this heart would accuse LOVE of enabling and validating harmful actions each time LOVE chooses not to impose punishment or consequences. The fear-infused heart believes that only the threat of punishment can rein in the self-absorbed, shortsighted, and destructive choices we see others make or secretly would make ourselves. From its perspective, only negative consequences can restrain the dominating, grasping, lying, and controlling expressions of destructive fear. These fear-distorted beliefs and the distrust they foster eventually blind the hardened heart's bearer to all the accompanying destructive consequences of its actions. It cannot and does not trust, and its own distrustfulness makes its bearer an unworthy candidate for the trust of others.

> The hardened heart cannot and does not trust, and its own distrustfulness makes its bearer an unworthy candidate for the trust of others.

The love-infused perspective sees the purpose within LOVE's grace. Grace is extended, inviting its intended recipients to step back on the path of trust. When grace is given despite the harmfulness of an action, this is not a tacit endorsement of that injurious action. This gracing action is a validation of the graced recipient's personhood, exercising belief in the person they can be going forward. With this gift, LOVE is creating a safe space where imperfection, failures, and intentional and unintentional acts of harm can be revealed—but then transformed—in the safety and security of LOVE.

This safe space allows the harming person to confront the full and ever-widening destructiveness of their choices while acknowledging responsibility for their harms. At the same time, this grace-filled space encourages this person to seek the healing grace needed for repairing and making meaningful restitution for those inflicted harms. LOVE is preparing the now graced person for trustworthiness.

Those who live in the awareness that they are the recipients of undeserved forgiveness are also more sensitive to their own potential harmfulness; paradoxically, they are less likely to be harmful in their future actions. Anyone who steps into this safe space of grace will be transformed, humbled, and made ready for a different and more empathetic quality of relationship. The revealing self-disclosure and transparency made possible here recreates the more trustworthy partners needed for the Giving Creator's intended dance of giving, receiving, and giving again with trust.

Revealing with Trust

Stepping into this safe space created by LOVE and revealing our real selves is still a choice of trust. Objective, big-picture logic might recognize the benefits of a wider world where trust and trustworthiness are the norm, but our participation with our own trusting steps continually faces relentless challenges. In addition to the already noted resistances to grace, the destructive fear within us deflects both our awareness of our fear and our consciousness of its destructive effects.

Destructive fear's reasonable-sounding but deceptive questions exploit our insecurities and would distract us from or delay our steps of trust. Fear would have us ask, "Are there not real risks in revealing my imperfections, my failures, and my ongoing neediness for healing grace? Would it not feel safer to keep up the façade that I am self-sufficient and can handle everything on my own?"

> "Would it not feel safer to keep up the façade that I am self-sufficient and can handle everything on my own?"

This resistance due to the fear within us is powerful and compelling. The destructive fear originating in our attempts toward living outside the Creator's gifting limits is not only terrified by the prospect of vulnerability and neediness, but also makes every effort to avoid them. This fear within us generates unlimited insecurity, unlimited wants, unlimited capacity for lying, and an unlimited need for control. It also wreaks havoc in our lives and relationships, producing a whole new dimension of vulnerability and angst.

Destructive fear is always cultivating hurtfulness, enticing us to hold tightly to what we have. It obscures our own truth, discouraging truthfulness in our self-presentation to others while encouraging additional manipulations and efforts to impose control. If we were seeing the hurtful impact of our words and actions with complete clarity, it would be illuminating. Seeing this and the way our tight hold restricts our capacity for receiving new gifts would be frightening as well. We could never quantify the time and energy wasted while we are maintaining false images covering lies or blocking freedom, healing and reconciling opportunities with our controlling choices. If we were to recognize the full impact of destructive fear and its devastating influence on the choices we make, we would also have to face both the all-encompassing nature of our vulnerability to it and the overwhelming shame, guilt, and powerlessness it leaves in its wake.

For all these reasons, it generally seems easier in the moment to deny the presence of destructive fear and its role in the vulnerability, discomfort, and hurt it both generates and exposes. This denial insulates us. At least for that moment, it appears to protect us from distress. But like the practicing addict, denying their own powerlessness and thereby avoiding what would be the first step (of the 12 Steps) in their own healing recovery, we are denying the power that destructive fear is exercising in our lives and relationships.

Continuing in denial only adds to the problem. Any time we are unwilling to see, name, and acknowledge the destructive forces in our lives, we only feed their power, trapping ourselves more tightly in their grasp. This reality-resisting stance prevents our discovering the very help we need. As long as we insist on being "lone rangers" and doing battle with these unseen but powerfully influential forces on our own, we are doomed to fail against them. We will continue being trapped in the denial-perpetuating, self-made prisons we construct.

> As long as we insist on being "lone rangers" and doing battle with unseen but powerfully influential forces on our own, we are doomed to fail against them. We will continue being trapped in the denial-perpetuating, self-made prisons we construct.

Despite the continual pull of destructive fear drawing us toward this failing, denial-filled—but still often tried—strategy, LOVE seeks to break through the denial, inviting us to the light of honest self-disclosure and the trusting response of revealing love. With the transparent honesty of revealing love, we make the trusting step of revealing ourselves—warts and all—in the safety of the Giving Creator's LOVE. Stepping into this secure space of gracing light and acceptance, we can safely see, name, and acknowledge the destructive power of the many expressions of fear within our lives. We also clearly see our ongoing need for LOVE and the healing grace it imparts.

As we are seeing, naming, and acknowledging destructive fear's presence in our lives, we are also identifying all the places where we need grace and LOVE's healing. Within this safe space, hiding from fear and avoiding awareness of fear is no longer necessary. These concerns are swallowed up in the infinite vastness of gracing and healing LOVE. If we will listen and respond to LOVE and its grace-empowered perspective, our relationship with destructive fear and the vulnerability it dreads will radically change. As we are residing in the security of LOVE, we can embrace both vulnerability and neediness, recognizing in these the life-giving triggers for releasing the healing grace we need. Where we have need and when we have need, we find grace supplied for meeting the need.

The grace that many people find in 12-Step recovery illustrates this connection between honest self-disclosure, healing grace, and the resulting transformation. 12-Step recoveries begin with the addicts' admission of powerlessness and inability to manage their addiction. This humble admission of each recovering addict initiates the willingness to reach outside for help that can be found in a Higher Power and the larger recovering community. The gracing acceptance, reciprocating self-disclosure, and ongoing encouragement for staying on a path of rigorous honesty and personal responsibility produce positive shifts in the character and trustworthiness of the ones faithfully applying the 12-Steps. The supportive community found in 12-Step groups then becomes its own tangible source of ongoing grace for those both learning to trust and striving to be more worthy of trust.

Practicing Revealing Love

If we are making our individual response of revealing love, we willingly self-disclose, taking responsibility for the person we are and what we have done. Perhaps the first and most basic confession is an acknowledgment of the "two things"—"there is a God and I am not God." This confession of our basic humanness acknowledges our subordinated relationship to the Giving Creator, highlighting our ongoing dependence upon our Creator for the wisdom, courage, and sustaining love needed for addressing and meeting our physical, emotional, and spiritual needs. We are recognizing that the Creator's gifts have given us life, imagination, and the freedom of choosing but also a freedom for making choices contrary to the Creator's original intention. Have we been aligning our choices with the intentional purposes of the Creator, or have we chosen to live outside these and gone our own way?

We have often gone our own way. Our expressions of revealing love freely acknowledge this reality, facing and taking ownership for our self-focused, hurtful actions and the consequences following them. Hiding behind destructive fear's influence on our wayward actions might be tempting, but the confessions of revealing love exercise the open and straightforward approach, acknowledging our role in both activating and feeding the fear within us. We have made ongoing choices of listening to and collaborating with its urgings.

Our response of revealing love humbly admits our personal powerlessness over the all-encompassing expressions of destructive fear, emphasizing our absolute dependence upon the forgiveness, acceptance, and transformative grace found in the Giving Creator's LOVE. This humble, vulnerable, and dependent response runs counter to everything destructive fear would demand of us, but it also releases us from the hold that fear has on us. If we have owned our personal responsibility, exposed our own weaknesses, and admitted our need for help, we have already given away the very vulnerabilities that destructive fear would normally exploit and use as primary weapons against us. Fear cannot threaten us when deprived of ammunition.

As a consequence, this transparent honesty within revealing love creates a wonderful paradox. Revealing our vulnerability and trusting the gracing power of LOVE is also disarming the power of coercive, destructive fear. Fear becomes powerless against

LOVE's noncoercive vulnerability. The transparency and vulnerability of LOVE conquers fear.

> Fear becomes powerless against LOVE's noncoercive vulnerability.

There are other life-giving benefits flowing naturally out of the transparent honesty we exercise with revealing love. Our response frees up energy we might have previously devoted toward denying, defending, and shifting blame for our actions. The Serenity Prayer speaks of "accepting the things we cannot change, [having] courage to change the things we can, and [having] the wisdom to know the difference." Accepting the realities about who we are and what we have done allows us to invest our energy in the things we actually can change.

Could we not work toward repairing the damage our destructive actions have caused, seeking ways of making restitution? Could we not allow the Creator's gracing LOVE to remake us from the inside out, transforming what we say and do? Could we not make every effort to be truly more worthy of the trust of others? LOVE is inviting us to be trustworthy partners in the dance of giving, receiving, and giving again with trust.

One of the key elements of trustworthiness is honesty. Other people cannot trust us if they cannot trust the truthfulness of what we say or do. Even trusting ourselves requires truthfulness with our own selves. Deception naturally fosters distrust. We cannot make a practice of deceiving others or ourselves without undermining our own capacity for trusting others or our ability to be a trustworthy person in our ongoing relationships.

But a delicate balance is required. The truthfulness that would promote trust must always be seasoned with grace and handled with wisdom and discernment. Without these tempering elements, truth can easily be converted into a weapon of hurtfulness. Is the "truth" I have actually true or merely speculation? Does it build up or tear down? Is this the time or place for sharing it? Is the recipient ready to hear this "truth"?

> The truthfulness that would promote trust must always be seasoned with grace and handled with wisdom and discernment. Without these tempering elements, truth can easily be converted into a weapon of hurtfulness.

As wisdom would teach us, we humans are more likely to hear and apply unpleasant truth if it is presented within a context of grace. Otherwise, we will instinctively deny, resist, and slip back into the familiar expressions of fear. LOVE helps us bridge these gaps. When the healing grace supplied by the Giving Creator is supplemented by personal expressions of safety-imparting grace, then a safe space is created, allowing each of us and those we touch to feel safe enough to hear, acknowledge, and apply this truth constructively.

While the Giving Creator initiates and supplies healing grace, our capacity for imparting grace to others is directly related to our own personal awareness of the undeserved grace we have received. Only a person who knows they are recipients of undeserved grace is able to bestow that same quality of grace on another. If we are to move further down the path of greater trustworthiness, then we must nurture not only a self-awareness of our weaknesses, failures, and defects of character but also keep retelling our own experiences with this healing grace that transforms them. There is a vast difference between one who is ignorant of both their shortcomings and need for grace and the knowing person who intimately identifies their flaws and failures, relying upon a trust that all of these are swallowed up in a boundless ocean of healing and undeserved grace.

Destructive fear would have us hide from this self-knowledge and deny the possibility of grace. Knowing this, we must proactively counter a natural drift back into its trust-avoiding clutches. Intentional efforts toward recognizing and addressing this backsliding mindset of fear in its early stages can help us "nip it in the bud," choosing instead those countering practices that exercise trust.

When concerns about the shaming and discomforting aspects of a deeper search of our own selves might be frightening, we can embrace self-awareness, reminding ourselves that healing LOVE can redeem and transform anything that might be found within us. When tempted to take a closed or secretive stance to hide our real selves from others, we can instead practice openness and transparency, remembering that the Giving Creator of LOVE knows all our secrets but still supports and believes in the person we can become. These trusting self-reminders allow us to re-enter the healing space where we can safely explore any revealed concerns while freeing us to look for and find all the wondrous but yet undiscovered gifts residing within us.

The trust-filled and honest transparency flowing out of our exercise of revealing love enlarges our capacity for trustworthiness. Seeing and naming the destructive forces in our lives (both realized and potential), facing and taking ownership of our self-focused, hurtful actions and their consequences, and recognizing and mourning the wounding impact of our actions on others all prepare us for receiving the forgiveness, acceptance, and transformative grace found in the Giving Creator's LOVE. This grace-filled progression imparts the genuine humility, vulnerability, and sense of empathy that would make us worthy of greater trust.

As our personal awareness and appreciation for the potential good or ill within us all is wedded to a consciousness of the ongoing experience of redeeming and transforming grace, we become more safe and trustworthy participants within all our relationships. Perhaps Jesus had something like this in mind when he instructed his disciples to be "wise as serpents and innocent as doves" (Matt. 10:16b).

Embracing vulnerability and the growth of our trustworthiness frees us to be vulnerable and welcoming in our approach to others. Revealing love also permits us to let go of the self-protective and guarded defensiveness prompting us to hold so tightly to what we possess. The transparent honesty of revealing love prepares us for another healing response of trust: the generosity of giving love.

Questions for Reflection

1. If you believe that "we are always within one step of getting back on the path of trust" and that LOVE "continually speaks words of boundless grace," how does this change your view of the present and future? What does this mean for your self-image and sense of self-worth?
2. What impedes your own reception of grace? What steps might you take to grow your capacity to trust grace?
3. Describe experiences where you had a need, reached outside yourself for help, and received assistance that met your need. What feelings did you have at the time? What are your feelings about the experience now?
4. What personal shortcomings or vulnerabilities might you self-disclose that would help others trust you more? What impact might a deeper level of trust have on the authenticity of those individual relationships going forward?

A Window from Scripture

A Parable of Forgiveness
(Matt. 18:21-35)

How much are we obligated to forgive? When can we say "enough" and walk away from those who have betrayed us, injured us, or disappointed us multiple times?

> Then Peter came and said to him, "Lord, if another member of the church sins against me, how often should I forgive? As many as seven times?" Jesus said to him, "Not seven times, but, I tell you, seventy-seven times.

> "For this reason the kingdom of heaven may be compared to a king who wished to settle accounts with his slaves. When he began the reckoning, one who owed him ten thousand talents was brought to him; and, as he could not pay, his lord ordered him to be sold, together with his wife and children and all his possessions, and payment to be made. So the slave fell on his knees before him, saying, 'Have patience with me, and I will pay you everything.' And out of pity for him, the lord of that slave released him and forgave him the debt. But that same slave, as he went out, came upon one of his fellow slaves who owed him a hundred denarii; and seizing him by the throat, he said, 'Pay what you owe.' Then his fellow slave fell down and pleaded with him, 'Have patience with me, and I will pay you.' But he refused; then he went and threw him into prison until he would pay the debt. When his fellow slaves saw what had happened, they were greatly distressed, and they went and reported to their lord all that had taken place. Then his lord summoned him and said to him, 'You wicked slave! I forgave you all that debt because you pleaded with me. Should you not have had mercy on your fellow slave, as I had mercy on you?' And in anger his lord handed him over to be tortured until he would pay his entire debt. So my heavenly Father will also do to every one of you, if you do not forgive your brother or sister from your heart."

Peter recognized that forgiveness is commendable for people of faith, but are there not limits upon its practice? He offered what he probably considered a generous accommodation—seven times. Jesus' response of "seventy-seven times" is followed by a parable, revealing a paradigm-shifting understanding of forgiveness.

With this understanding, forgiveness is not so much a task we do; it is a living reflection of an embraced, trusting, and transformative relationship with the Giver of gracing LOVE. Rather than focusing on the betrayal, injury, or disappointment we think we "ought" to "forgive," this quality of forgiveness focuses on the undeserved and gracing LOVE that has already forgiven us for our own injurious acts and betrayals. As we make room for this gracing LOVE, a real and heartfelt forgiveness naturally flows out of us, changing us and transforming our relationships with those needing our forgiveness.

Jesus' parable tells the story of a king settling accounts with his servants. One man owes the king an astronomical personal debt—whole nations would struggle in repaying the sum. When the king orders this man, his family, and all he has to be sold to pay off the debt, the man begs for more time, promising to pay back everything he owes. Despite the utter impossibility of this man's ever making good on this promise, the gracing king has pity, canceling the entirety of the debt and letting him go free. In the economy of Jesus' story, no debt—whatever its size—is beyond the forgiving power of LOVE.

There is one qualification, however. Our capacity for receiving the fullness of this healing grace is determined by our own grace-inspired willingness to extend that same grace to others. Grace is bestowed so it can be shared and given again. If we try hoarding it for ourselves, we divert and squander its healing power, activating instead our own self-imposed incarceration into a torturing prison of destructive fear.

We see this sobering reality play out in this first man's response to his fellow servant in need of grace: he showed no mercy, throwing the fellow servant into prison. Perhaps this first man had only experienced the relief of avoiding unwanted consequences. Perhaps he felt the disdainful sense of superiority of one believing he has hoodwinked a foolish creditor. But his denying of grace to his fellow servant reveals he certainly did not experience the sense of undeserved, healing grace that brings humility, transformation, and the confirmation of real forgiveness.

Any time we truly experience this grace-filled quality of real forgiveness, it creates within us a sense of joyful indebtedness to the Giver of grace. When experiencing this true forgiveness, this "grace debt" is not a burden but a further source of joy. We gladly repay it by paying (giving) grace forward to those needing it.

This first man had incurred a "grace debt," but refusing to pay grace forward to his fellow servant in need set in motion his own self-imposed imprisonment of graceless self-torture. The Giver of grace may be the source of all we give, inspiring and enabling us to give, but we are never compelled or forced to give. True giving and true forgiveness are always freely chosen—from the heart. As a respecter of our freedom, LOVE will always allow our choosing not to give, even letting us experience the torturous consequences of that choice.

The gracing king's "anger" in the parable was thus a heartfelt response to the opportunities missed and joy deferred while this first servant continued to maintain his graceless stance toward those in need around him. The first servant's experience of "punishment" was completely self-inflicted. It would end the very moment he freely chose to pay the "grace debt" forward, extending grace and forgiveness from his own heart to his brother or sister.

And so it is for each of us. The forgiveness we extend to others is a barometer, revealing the depth of grace we have both been given and received. Do we choose to remain in self-imposed prisons of held grudges and poisonous unforgiveness, or are we able to step out in trust, acknowledging the enormity of our own forgiven debt and forgiving our brothers and sisters from the heart? Each day, each moment, we decide.

Chapter 9
Transforming Grasping Fear with Giving Love

Recognizing Giftedness

Being human is an amazing gift! The experiencing of LOVE reshapes our understanding of human giftedness and our relationship with the Giving Creator who freely gives. LOVE softens our hearts when we respond with a step forward on the path of trust. Each step increases our capacity for seeing, experiencing, and trusting LOVE.

This softer heart and wider vision is transformative. Within the freeing security of gracing LOVE, responses of submitting love and revealing love empower our recognition of the widespread actualized giftedness and potential giftedness all around us. We see that the purposeful gifts of the Creator do not stand in isolation but also contain their own seeds for further gifting, only awaiting our grace-inspired, trusting, and partnering actions to bear fruit.

LOVE removes the veil, letting us see all the richness within the gifts and blessings themselves, in addition to the life-giving (but humbling) realization that we are the undeserving recipients of all we continue receiving. When we are looking through LOVE's life-enhancing lens, we clearly see the widening spectrum of our blessings, experiencing the additional blessing of knowing we are blessed. Recognizing the initiating, empowering, and sustaining role of the Giving Creator of LOVE that brings this incomprehensible blessing inspires another grace-gift: gratitude.

Gratitude is a multifaceted, multidimensional grace-gift, providing an essential dance-step that initiates our participation in the dance of giving, receiving, and giving again with trust. With gratitude, grace and trust join together in a life-giving and transformative collaboration. Gratitude may be experienced in the present moment, but its reach and influence extend all along the time continuum, reframing the way we see and understand the whole of our past, present, and future. How do we progress from recognizing the giftedness all around us to experiencing and expressing our personal gratitude?

> How do we progress from recognizing the giftedness all around us to experiencing and expressing our personal gratitude?

Gratitude can eventually become our freely exercised choice, but it initially comes to us as another gift of LOVE. Just as with our exercise of submitting love and revealing love, gratitude originates as a grace-empowered leap of faith. As the initiator and fuel for all these trusting practices, LOVE also stands ready, assisting us as we exercise willingness to take gratitude's trusting leap.

LOVE's offer of help brings a cumulative benefit. Since the trust we exercise in any one of these dimensions naturally spills over into the other areas, LOVE's "leap" assistance into gratitude gives us one more way of hearing the invitation and joining in the trust-filled dance. Individually and collectively, each of these expressions of trust give us the opportunity for becoming co-creators and participants in this mutually reinforcing, healing cycle of grace working through every trusting step we take.

Steps of trust are always associated with some dimension of vulnerability. While submitting love leaves us vulnerable to loss of control and revealing love exposes our weaknesses and shortcomings, gratitude and its close companion, giving love, highlight another vulnerability—an ongoing awareness of vulnerability. It is hard to separate gratitude from the continuing acknowledgement that we live with the presence of constant need—physically, mentally, emotionally, and spiritually.

Moving into gratitude thereby sets us at odds with the fear-promoted worldview that would have us be self-contained and self-sufficient individuals, avoiding neediness or dependence upon anyone or anything outside ourselves. This fear-encouraged illusion feeds our egos with its appeal to a misplaced sense of self-importance. In actuality, it is building "castles in the sand," doing little to ground our being in values having substance, stability, or lasting value beyond our own selves.

Gratitude has a different worldview and affirms—perhaps even celebrates—the awareness that we are not self-contained, self-sufficient individuals and were never intended to be. With gratitude, we recognize that everything we have—at its core—is an unmerited gift of grace we hold in trust. Gratitude lets us clearly see the Giver behind this gifting, the purpose-filled nature of each gift, and the joyous invitation we now have for joining in with our trust-filled steps of participatory giving.

The logic of gratitude may seem compelling when we are viewing it through the life-giving lens of LOVE, but it is still up to us to make the grace-assisted leap of trust. LOVE will never coerce or compel our choice of gratitude; only our willful consent establishes its root in our lives. This movement into gratitude may be an active choice of embracing this life-giving spirit; it may be the more passive result of just relaxing our resistance to the giftedness all around us and letting gratitude fill the space with its healing grace. Whichever way we let gratitude permeate our worldview, its presence brings transformation and new freedom into our lives.

Unleashing Gratitude

Gratitude's immediate impact touches and transforms our relationship with the past. As an act of trust, gratitude naturally gives us a trust-filled perspective, helping us reframe the way we understand our past. There is a world of difference between framing our past experiences from the vantage point of blessing and viewing them through the distorted lens of entitlement.

An entitled perspective finds little room for lasting satisfaction in meaningful relationships, material holdings, or personal accomplishments. It understands these as our rightful possession or the just reward for our efforts. With a sense of entitlement, we take what we have for granted, looking forward to the next relationship, possession, or accomplishment we can obtain. This stance leaves us with a fleeting moment of satisfaction that soon passes as we move on to the next thing on our list. In contrast, viewing relationships, possessions, or accomplishments through the lens of gratitude lets us see each of these as the blessings and gifts they have been to us in the past while recognizing the ways these continue to bless us in the present and future.

Gratitude also helps us shift our interpretations of past mistakes and failures in a more life-giving direction. Just as a sense of entitlement distorts our sense of self with its misplaced emphasis on our own importance, so we can be led astray by an outsized focus on painful past events or regrettable actions we have inflicted on others or ourselves. Any time we allow particular life events or actions to be the definer for how we see ourselves, we generate a distorted self-image. As these misleading and incomplete self-definitions get intertwined with unresolved feelings of shame and guilt we associate with our regrettable experiences, we start viewing and interpreting the story of our lives through a very self-destructive lens.

> Any time we allow particular life events or actions to be the definer for how we see ourselves, we generate a distorted self-image.

There is certainly a place for taking personal responsibility for actions and events in our lives, but a more accurate accounting must also include the tempering recognition that our actions and the actions of others were part of a larger context. This larger context influenced the choices set before us at the time and all that happened in response. We may have indeed made decisions and done things that proved foolish, hurtful, and regrettable in the hindsight of the present, but each one had seemed reasonable to us in that fateful moment of action. Our fear-prompted insecurities can make it difficult to see and believe this more sympathetic narrative. Destructive fear pushes us to keep feeding the distortions and reinforcing the ever-narrowing, self-destructive storyline, making it hard to reach beyond ourselves for help.

Gratitude helps us disrupt this destructive process. With its focus and appreciation for giftedness all around us, it takes the attention off ourselves, recognizing the presence of a bigger picture influencing the things that happen and the choices we make. In concert with LOVE, gratitude softens our hearts and allows us to detach ourselves from the distorting self-definitions derived solely from our past actions.

> In concert with LOVE, gratitude softens our hearts and allows us to detach ourselves from the distorting self-definitions derived solely from our past actions.

We are indeed human and flawed, but we are still filled with great potential and opportunities for a hopeful future. Living out its trust-filled openness to the assistance of LOVE, gratitude moves us toward forgiving ourselves as we embrace our real selves with all our flaws and potential. Having gratitude helps us extend a gracing and healing perspective toward everyone we encounter.

Gratitude can also help us reframe our understanding of past losses. When we experience losses, it seems natural to focus exclusively on what has been taken away or the future opportunities missed. Not only fueling a resentment that keeps us stuck in the past, this focus inhibits us from recognizing the gifts we still have and enjoy. Gratitude lets us see even our losses as blessings we can celebrate going forward. With this reframing, gratitude lightens and lifts the grief-filled burden we often associate with the losses we experience, replacing it with a deepened appreciation for each meaning-filled gift we have had the opportunity of sharing. This shift in perspective is not denying us the sadness and painful emotions that naturally attend our losses but is supplying richer context for these emotions in their ongoing work of healing our grief.

In my community, we have a parent-led support group for parents who have been impacted by a miscarriage, stillbirth, or early infancy loss. This group offers a monthly support meeting for parents who have newly experienced a loss and also an annual remembrance service where each family can hear their baby's name read aloud, light a candle, and celebrate anew the gift of their child. Inspired by their love for the child they lost years before, the parent leaders of this group respond by giving back, assisting others who are newly hurting. While freshly grieving parents certainly benefit from the compassion and grief education they experience through the group, the leaders themselves find ongoing healing for their own grief as they live out their gratitude for their child by serving the group.

The healing we find through gratitude not only transforms our perceptions of our losses, but also promotes an ever-deepening appreciation for the bountiful gifts we currently enjoy and the Giver who continues providing them. As a chaplain (and a human being), I am grateful for those who teach me daily about the life-giving power of gratitude as they employ it in their life challenges. Gratitude really does make a difference.

Gratitude transforms our perception and experience of our past, changing our outlook on our present and future. Freed from a focus on unredeemable past failures and the weight of unresolved grief, gratitude's concentration upon the blessings surrounding us naturally fills us with a heartfelt joy. Recognizing LOVE's ongoing provision of blessing with abundance, gratitude undermines the fear-derived "scarcity mindset" with all its attendant expectation that there can never be enough. It promotes an "abundance mindset" that trusts the Giver's faithfulness in providing for every need. Gratitude's transforming of our past, present, and future; our recognizing of the Giver behind this worldview of blessing; and our trusting in the abundant supply of our needs all combine in calling forth the responses of our trusting expressions of giving love.

Giving Love

All our expressions of giving love are a natural response to the many gifts of LOVE, but gratitude remains the first step and an essential component in each of them, infusing them with its freeing and joyous spirit. If grace is the currency of LOVE in the trusting dance, then gratitude and our expressions of giving love would be the coinage we use for paying grace forward and joining in this dance ourselves.

An atmosphere of celebration and joy accompanies each responding expression of giving love. The Giver's gracing LOVE is making available the grace needed for transforming the distorted expectations, regrettable actions, and difficult losses of our past. When LOVE gives us new hope for the present and future, it naturally calls forth responses of giving love. With each gift of LOVE, we are receiving tools for disarming and reframing destructive fear's grasping behavioral attitudes and all the insecurities it exploits.

Two of these destructive behavioral attitudes—bitterness and resentment—are often found together and seem to feed off each other. Both find fertile soil when we forget the wisdom of "I am not God" and cultivate instead the illusion that the world is supposed to be revolving around me and my wants and desires. Once we buy into these two false assumptions, we can find a never-ending pool of events and circumstances justifying our resentments. Did my achievement go unrecognized? Was favoritism shown to someone else? Did someone use me, manipulate me, or take advantage of me? Once self-absorbed bitterness and resentment take root, they poison all they touch, fostering and fueling sarcasm, cynicism, and a sense of suspiciousness that destroys from within, consuming the person that holds them.

Bitterness and resentment are also energizers of the retaliatory hurtful actions we direct toward our perceived inflictors of harm. Rationalizing our vengeful conduct seems logical when the caustic venom of these two is poisoning our minds. We may direct their venom inwardly or outwardly, but with them we are causing untold destruction in our relationships with others and with our own selves. Harboring these comes easily; getting rid of them is another story.

Neither our direct efforts nor self-imposed lectures are effective in banning or extinguishing them. Bitterness and resentment seem to feed and grow off these attentions and draw strength from our battles to dislodge them. Increasing our efforts only entrenches them more deeply into our lives.

If trying not to be bitter or resentful does not work, how do we get off this reactive, self-perpetuating, and relationally destructive treadmill, changing its recipe for hurt? There is only one viable alternative: the path of *trust-filled acceptance*. This pathway was introduced in earlier discussions as a way of maintaining a fruitful partnership between knowledge and imagination, but this proactive exercise of acceptance also demonstrates an expression of giving love.

Trust-filled acceptance brings freeing hope, addressing bitterness and resentment at their source. Trusting in the security of LOVE and incorporating the gift-seeing properties of gratitude, this accepting response freely acknowledges that "I am not God," embracing the limitations of our humanness. This response recognizes and accepts that having "whatever I want whenever I want it" is not within my power and would not serve my best interest even if it were. With its corresponding openness to newness and gift, trust-filled acceptance redirects our focus from commiserating about what we cannot change to devoting our energies toward changing what can be changed for the better. This shift in focus not only reverses the direction of those thoughts fueling bitterness and resentments, but it also replaces them with ones encouraging us to build relationships of growing trust.

> Trust-filled acceptance not only reverses the direction of those thoughts fueling bitterness and resentments, but it also replaces them with ones encouraging us to build relationships of growing trust.

Trust-filled acceptance offers multiple benefits that encourage a sense of hopefulness about the future. It also faces a constant countering flow of cultural pressures and societal expectations discouraging us from its practice. The insistence of messages urging us toward acquiring more for ourselves and seeing possessions as measures of our worth are bombarding us from every direction and distorting our view of the world and everything in it—including ourselves.

While we are entrapped in a self-made prison of acquisition and possessiveness, this thought may seem counterintuitive—but less is more. Letting go and giving provide freedom and release. There is a delight-filled paradox: the more we let go and the more we generously give, the more we expand our capacity both to receive and to give again.

Letting go and giving—these two proactive expressions of giving love—join trust-filled acceptance in reflecting the "abundance mindset" that expresses confidence in the Giver's faithful provision of our needs. As we practice letting go and as we exercise acts of giving, we are reframing our relationship with possessions, disarming the insecurities that would fuel the drive to acquire more and grip tightly. Both of these proactive choices take their cue from LOVE and build upon the trust expressed through trust-filled acceptance. They mirror a paradigm-shifting change in our source of self-valuing and sense of security.

As we practice these choices and trust in the Giver's provision of our needs, our actions profess that our sense of security is no longer dependent upon the breadth of our personal possessions or our ability to safeguard them. These trust-filled changes release us from the tyranny of constantly needing to compare our holdings to those of others and the competitive conflicts arising from these comparisons. As gratitude reminds us that all we have is a gift, we find freedom from the entangling burdens of an ownership mentality. We instead become stewards who apportion and share our gifts in concert with LOVE. As we allow the generosity of this gracing LOVE to flow through us, other gifts formerly held in bondage to our grasping mentality can be released, freeing us for fuller participation in the Giver's dance of giving, receiving, and giving again with trust.

Countering Unforgiveness

Perhaps the most destructive behavioral attitude held in bondage to our grasping mentality is unforgiveness. Unlike the bitterness and resentment that often have a more general and globalized focus, each instance of unforgiveness is inherently personal. It has a specific target and remains ever mindful of the particular perceived hurtful actions or betrayals energizing it. While withholding forgiveness can certainly be harmful to the one being targeted by its negative energy, its greatest destructive impact seems reserved for the one doing the withholding.

> While withholding forgiveness can certainly be harmful to the one being targeted by its negative energy, its greatest destructive impact seems reserved for the one doing the withholding.

As Jesus' parable of forgiveness teaches, our individual practice of unforgiveness carries its own dire consequences and sets in motion a self-imposed imprisonment of graceless self-torture. Experience also teaches that unforgiveness has a poisoning effect on our capacity and availability for healthy relationships. When we withhold forgiveness in one relationship, it erects barriers of guardedness and suspicion that filter into every other relationship—even those that would seemingly have no connection. We will find it hard, if not impossible, to maintain full openness and transparency in any of our relationships while still harboring unforgiveness in one of them.

Unforgiveness has other destructive consequences that handicap our experience of the present and future. Withholding forgiveness keeps us stuck in an unchangeable past, locking us into patterns of relating that maintain old conflicts. Unforgiveness may also create the conditions for new and "justified" acts of retaliation, extending these unresolvable conflicts into the foreseeable future. As these dysfunctional patterns play out, the destructiveness of unforgiveness can swallow up future generations in its wake. How can we reverse this destructive tide and find restoration and reconciliation?

While the obvious cure for unforgiveness would be a spirit of forgiveness, we cannot manufacture this spirit on our own. Our self-generated (and often guilt-laden) efforts at this produce a poor substitute for real forgiveness. Indeed, a counterfeit "forgiveness" may extend the patterns of destruction. How many times have we been "forgiven" and yet felt that the forgiver was still holding us hostage and keeping us in their debt? This "forgiveness" does little to bring healing and may actually drive a deeper wedge between the parties.

This counterfeit "forgiveness" is a product of personal insecurities and efforts to avoid vulnerability. It manipulates power relationships so the one who "forgives" is able to maintain a position of self-righteous moral superiority and the other is left to carry their own burden of shame, guilt, and sense of inferiority alone. Not only does this push the originating hurt further beneath the surface where it remains unresolved and continues resurfacing, but it also keeps both parties stuck in a relational pattern that alienates them from each other, disconnecting them from essential truths about themselves.

The "self-righteous" one is not always so righteous as he or she might want to assert, and the "forgiven" one is not as unrighteous in every moment. Both parties are human and subject to the same limitations, gifts, and potential that come with our common humanity. Unfortunately, this manipulative, often guilt-laden, but ultimately ineffective form of "forgiveness" is all too common. It undermines lasting trust and fails to bring about the healing transformation we need.

In contrast, the real forgiveness that expresses giving love brings reconnection and healing, touching everyone within its sphere of influence. Unlike the counterfeit form of forgiveness, this life-giving forgiveness is not something we manufacture or initiate on our own; its source is the ever-giving and abundant flow of LOVE. When we recognize (with LOVE's assistance) that we are the continually undeserving recipients of an ever-flowing flood of gracing forgiveness for our own failures and shortcomings, we naturally perceive and interpret both the hurtful acts themselves and the ones who acted hurtfully toward us in a different way.

Transforming Grasping Fear with Giving Love

> When we recognize with LOVE's assistance that we are the continually undeserving recipients of an ever-flowing flood of gracing forgiveness for our own failures and shortcomings, we naturally perceive and interpret both the hurtful acts themselves and the ones who acted hurtfully toward us in a different way.

We may still see the hurtfulness we received from the other, but we also see the wider context of hurt, woundedness, and insecurity triggering the other's hurtful action. This wider view helps us separate the hurtful action from the person who acted hurtfully. As we integrate this love-inspired transformation in perception and interpretation, we are free to reframe our response to the other and apply the same grace we have received for our wrongs to those who have wronged us. The surrounding security of the Giver's gracing LOVE creates a safe zone, leveling the ground between the wounded one and the one who did the wounding. Within this transformative space, true reconciliation and healing become possible.

> The surrounding security of the Giver's gracing LOVE creates a safe zone, leveling the ground between the wounded one and the one who did the wounding. Within this transformative space, true reconciliation and healing become possible.

This transforming grace and forgiveness surely benefits the one we forgive, but its greatest benefit may be reserved for us as forgivers. Not only do we as forgivers experience the joy of LOVE's healing for our own shortcomings, but we also can participate in the joy available to the one being released from their hurtful act. Since real forgiveness releases both the forgiver and the forgiven from the hurtful act bringing alienation, it allows for establishing together a new and safer relationship going forward. Any relationship built on real forgiveness would naturally be infused with the heartfelt gratitude, humility, and empathy we need for trustworthy connections.

This vision of transforming forgiveness may sound too good to be true. Are there not injuries and betrayals so heinous and terrible that they are beyond the power of real forgiveness to heal? Are there not those who would refuse our heartfelt forgiveness, deny their own hurtfulness, and willingly hurt and betray us again? Common sense would certainly nurture these doubts, and our observations of the world around us might confirm them. Can this transformative forgiveness really work in our world?

A transforming forgiveness only works when we factor in the unending, unlimited grace supplied by the Giver of healing LOVE. The full actualization of this life-giving forgiveness remains dependent upon our own willingness to trust LOVE and allow the healing power of this grace to work in us and through us. Since LOVE will never compel our trust or coerce our participation in the work of forgiveness, this leaves open the possibility that our inaction or lack of trust may place unnecessary limits on the healing power of forgiveness. Fortunately, despite our oft-too-frequent, forgiveness-limiting deficiencies in trust, LOVE is persistently inviting, empowering, and making possible the deeper levels of humility, openness, and trust within us that would allow the flow of healing grace to come through us to others.

With LOVE's assistance, our giving love responses of gratitude, trust-filled acceptance, generous giving, and life-giving forgiveness bring opportunity to join in the Creator's trust-filled dance in new and deeper ways. As we exercise the freedom coming with the release from grasping expressions of fear, this generosity of giving love is also preparing us for the self-giving, sacrificial responses of serving love. In the next chapter, we will examine serving love and the ways it addresses and transforms the dominating expressions of destructive fear.

Questions for Reflection

1. How has your gratitude (or lack thereof) altered your understanding of your past or your hopes for the future? What influence does gratitude play in your life right now?
2. What past relationships, losses, or memories of your own actions could benefit from an infusion of gratitude? What are you giving up when you choose a path of gratitude?
3. What are your own personal barriers to practicing trust-filled acceptance? What fears hinder your letting go?
4. In what relationships have you withheld forgiveness in the past? What enabled you to move toward forgiving? Where might you be withholding forgiveness now?
5. What challenges do you face in forgiving yourself? How does trusting LOVE's grace help in addressing these challenges?

A Window from Scripture

Redefining "Greatness"
(Mark 9:33-37, 10:42-45)

Who is the greatest? The disciples' question to one another is the question haunting every generation. Is not the greatest the one who rules, who has authority, who is the first among many? Is it not the one who has the power to influence, command, and dominate everyone else? And who is the least—the child, the servant, the vulnerable, the powerless? At its core, the disciples' question is about power—who has it and (perhaps more importantly) how does one get it and keep it for oneself?

> Then they came to Capernaum; and when he was in the house he asked them, "What were you arguing about on the way?" But they were silent, for on the way they had argued with one another who was the greatest. He sat down, called the twelve, and said to them, "Whoever wants to be first must be last of all and servant of all." Then he took a little child and put it among them; and taking it in his arms, he said to them, "Whoever welcomes one such child in my name welcomes me, and whoever welcomes me welcomes not me but the one who sent me"
>
> So Jesus called them and said to them, "You know that among the Gentiles those whom they recognize as their rulers lord it over them, and their great ones are tyrants over them. But it is not so among you; but whoever wishes to become great among you must be your servant, and whoever wishes to be first among you must be slave of all. For the Son of Man came not to be served but to serve, and to give his life a ransom for many."

Jesus turns these common assumptions about power upside down. In his community of grace, the one who aspires to be first lives it out by being the very last, and the one who would be great practices this by being a servant. Genuine humility and joyful service are the characterizing interactions within the community. This community is inclusive and welcoming to any and all who would receive its grace.

A special welcome is reserved for children. Challenging societal beliefs that devalued children for their dependency, vulnerability, and status among the "least," Jesus recognizes in children the embodiment of key elements within the gracing community—trust, openness, spontaneity, and giving. Only those with these childlike qualities can trustingly receive and give again the healing and gracing LOVE.

Jesus practiced what he preached, living out his words with his actions. He engaged the disciples while sitting down, showing them through this simple physical action a willingness to get down on their level—not using dominating authority and speaking down to them. Jesus demonstrated his welcome to children by bringing a child into the group and taking the child into his arms. Just prior to his crucifixion and death, Jesus took off his outer clothing, wrapped a towel around his waist, and washed the feet of each disciple. This was a concrete demonstration of gracing LOVE and his own serving spirit (see John 13:1-17). Each of these actions were foreshadowing Jesus' greatest act of service—fulfilling his promised destiny of life-giving service through giving his own life in the service of gracing LOVE.

What might be our response to Jesus' invitation to join his community of grace? If we seriously consider the Christian faith's assertion that Jesus was and is God in human flesh, then Jesus' actions embody an expression of the Creator's very character, providing a window into understanding this giving Creator's intended design for the universe. How would our trusting from this faith-filled vantage point shift our own priorities and actions? Would we be willing to lower ourselves, embrace the qualities of openness and humility, and give ourselves in welcoming service? Jesus' invitation to join this community of grace continues to be available to us all.

Chapter 10
Transforming Dominating Fear with Serving Love

Choosing Vulnerability

Being human is an amazing gift! As we make our individual trusting steps of submitting love, revealing love, and giving love, we are also opening ourselves to an enlarging spectrum of special gifts that LOVE makes available. When each special gift given is received and given again, transformation happens.

The trusting expectation that the Giver of LOVE is present with us in all circumstances brings freedom and inner security. The honest self-disclosure and transparency made possible by our responses to this gracing LOVE cultivates trustworthiness in us, allowing us to develop deeper and more meaningful relationships. Openness to the practice of gratitude and forgiveness offers a renewing and transforming perspective on our world and the lives we live. Each of these special gifts brings deeper spiritual life; each also extends beyond the Giving Creator's universally bestowed gifts—life, consciousness, imagination, choice-making capacity, and human limitation.

These special and spiritually enlarging gifts are certainly available to all, but they can only be received as we make trusting (but still LOVE-assisted) steps of collaboration with the Giving Creator of LOVE. Here again, we see the intertwining connections between vulnerability, trust, and the reception of grace. Each step of trust is a step into vulnerability and the leaving of our "comfort zone," but grace also seems to come to us and be received by us most freely when we are choosing to embrace our vulnerability. Unless we expose our willingness to trust and respond to LOVE, these available and special gifts remain unopened—we miss out on the joy and purposefulness they contain.

All trusting responses to LOVE require vulnerability. Our trust-filled steps of submitting, revealing, and giving love cannot be made without an accompanying willingness to be defenseless and exposed. But serving love necessitates an even more vulnerable vulnerability.

In submitting, revealing, and giving love, we are exposing vulnerabilities that merely represent us—elements or things we attribute to ourselves or about ourselves. With serving love, our exposed vulnerability is our very self. The distinction could be likened to the differing contributions of the hen and the pig to the farmer's breakfast of eggs and bacon: The hen gives from herself; the pig gives his very self. Serving love is self-giving and self-sacrificing. It might include vulnerabilities exposed by the other responses to LOVE but extends beyond them. As Jesus said in John 15:13, "No one has greater love than this, to lay down one's life for one's friends." The sacrificial vulnerability of serving love requires the highest level of trust.

> The sacrificial vulnerability of serving love requires the highest level of trust.

This deeper level of trust and the willingness to give vulnerably of ourselves is not something we can manufacture on our own. Giving vulnerably goes against all our natural instincts crying out for self-protectiveness and self-preservation. Only a constant resupply of LOVE can empower each and every self-chosen, ongoing step we make in the vulnerable dance of giving, receiving, and giving again with trust.

As we willingly receive the gifting of LOVE, allow it to pass through us to those who need it, and add our own gifting contributions to the mix, then our freely chosen responses of serving love find expression. The openness, vulnerability, and wholehearted compassion of our actions might appear effortless to an outside observer, but this is only because our ultimate source for each self-giving act is the Giving Creator of LOVE. Our grace-empowered trust finds security in the trustworthiness of LOVE, allowing us to be defenseless and exposed without needing to be afraid. LOVE drives out destructive fear, securing us as we are living out vulnerable trust.

> LOVE drives out destructive fear,
> securing us as we are living out vulnerable trust.

LOVE empowers the embracing of our personal vulnerability but also reaches out to those who are vulnerable around us. Similar to a magnet, LOVE draws our attention toward those in need and meets those needs through our responses of serving love. LOVE's initiating action unleashes a new and transformative dimension to the already familiar trust-filled dance.

As we join in and reach out to those in need, our responses of serving love become concrete expressions of gracing LOVE within those receiving them. In a real sense, our serving love responses embody LOVE to them. This gracing LOVE also comes back to us as we see LOVE embodied and revealed in the recipients of our serving love. In this dance of grace, LOVE passes through us, to another, back to us and back to others while transforming all who will trust LOVE's healing touch.

> In this dance of grace, LOVE passes through us, to another, back to us, and back to others while transforming all who will trust LOVE's healing touch.

Our responses of serving love may be active choices in the beginning, but with time this renewing flow can so transform us that our serving actions may not require conscious thought at all. These serving love responses become more than just actions we do—they become reflections of who we are. Once this happens, we may not even notice anything extraordinary or supernatural about the healing work of our actions. LOVE just naturally flows through us and from us to those who have need.

We see an example of this kind of unaware surprise in those who are affirmed and celebrated in Jesus' final parable in the gospel of Matthew. These commended ones saw needs in vulnerable persons and reached out to meet those needs. Unlike the all-too-commonly-observed charitable acts that are really about bringing attention to the giver, the "helpers" in Jesus' parable reached out with no expectation of being noticed by anyone. They acted out of serving love because they genuinely cared about the vulnerable and need-filled persons they encountered.

> Then the king [Jesus] will say to those at his right hand, 'Come, you that are blessed by my Father, inherit the kingdom prepared for you from the foundation of the world; for I was hungry and you gave me food, I was thirsty and you gave me something to drink, I was a stranger and you welcomed me, I was naked and you gave me clothing, I was sick and you took care of me, I was in prison and you visited me.' Then the righteous will answer him, 'Lord, when was it that we saw you hungry and gave you food, or thirsty and gave you something to drink? And when was it that we saw you a stranger and welcomed you, or naked and gave you clothing? And when was it that we saw you sick or in prison and visited you?' And the king will answer them, 'Truly I tell you, just as you did it to one of the least of these who are members of my family, you did it to me.'" (Matt. 25:34-40)

With this final parable, Jesus puts an exclamation point on his emphasis on identifying with the vulnerable. He so identifies with "the least of these" that his own presence comes to be embodied within them. How might this understanding change our perception of the vulnerable and needy around us? How might it shift our experiencing the neediness and vulnerability within ourselves?

If we believe Jesus' words, then serving the vulnerable is not an afterthought but the essential expression of serving love. Attending to needs and those with needs then becomes far more than just a part of living—it becomes the essence of living itself! As we integrate this understanding, we see that vulnerabilities and neediness are no longer liabilities or sources of shame; they are transformed into gifts, allowing our fuller participation in the dance of giving, receiving, and giving again with trust.

How then do we live out our serving love responses in our day-to-day lives? How do we reach out to the vulnerable within our sphere of influence? How do we attend to the broken places we find within ourselves?

Serving Love

Our responses of serving love are always empowered by LOVE, but we cannot overstate the importance of our own grace-assisted choices embracing both the vulnerability and brokenness we see in others and the vulnerable brokenness we find within our selves—embracing both dimensions is essential. Focusing solely on serving the vulnerability we see in others would not be sustainable. If we do not embrace our own vulnerabilities, our service to others naturally devolves into the condescending, paternalistic patterns of service that ultimately demean the "served" by robbing them of dignity and discounting their value as persons.

This half-hearted approach does not reflect serving love. It blocks our reception of the renewing flow of LOVE and puts us on a path to burnout and resentment. In contrast, when we embrace our personal brokenness and vulnerability, we are inviting the healing flood of grace-filled LOVE, receiving our own invitation to "Love the Lord your God with all your heart, and with all your soul, and with all your strength, and with all your mind; and your neighbor as yourself" (Luke 10:27).

Under the tutelage of LOVE, these words of Jesus are not so much a command to follow but an invitation into a whole new way of living and being. Our LOVE-assisted practice of loving God, loving others, and loving self then becomes another way of describing our own steps in the dance of giving, receiving, and giving again with trust. With every response of serving love, we are living this out—loving and embracing the vulnerability within others and ourselves, even as we are also loving and mirroring the vulnerability we see in the Giving Creator who practices a vulnerable trust in the creation. This love we are directing toward God, others, and ourselves returns to us again and again in an ever-growing, ever-empowering circle of life-giving grace.

> The love we are directing toward God, others, and ourselves returns to us again and again in an ever-growing, ever-empowering circle of life-giving grace.

This loving embrace of the vulnerability within others and ourselves qualitatively changes our interactions with the wider world. A growing sensitivity to brokenness and need helps us recognize the harm inflicted by fear-infused strategies that are using objectification, coercive power, and further exploitation as a norm. Looking to and experiencing the trustworthy backing of LOVE empowers us to meet objectification with person-valuing concern, coercive power with the moral authority of nonviolence, and exploitation with the willingness to stand with the exploited, speaking loving truth to the fear-filled purveyors of exploitation.

With these serving love responses, we are exercising a qualitatively different energy and power, embodying a "holy" anger rooted in LOVE that passionately believes in and seeks to bring out the highest and best within everyone it encounters. This LOVE-inspired anger fuels a healing spirit of self-giving and self-sacrifice, providing the necessary trustworthiness, gentle understanding, and courage required for undermining the rooting foundations of fear-derived actions and disarming them at their source.

The diplomatic movements of Mohandas Gandhi and Martin Luther King Jr. illustrate this. Influenced by the teachings of Jesus in the "Sermon on the Mount" about "turning the other cheek," "going the second mile," "loving your enemy," and "praying for persecutors" (see Matt. 5:38-44), these men and their followers courageously spoke truth to structural injustices of their society. Absorbing the violent blows of oppressors, they responded with a courageous pacifism, exposing the destructive fear within their persecutors even while communicating a LOVE that could awaken these to their better self and bring transformation. The hearts and attitudes of some were completely transformed in these encounters with the practitioners of nonaggressive engagement. The wider society experienced shifts that ultimately led to real changes in attitudes and laws, improving the lives of many and nudging justice a little closer to the realization of its ideals.

The benefit within this LOVE-empowered nonviolent approach may be evident but it still comes slowly and with many stops and starts—at times giving ground back or appearing to make little headway. As a consequence, it is tempting to abandon pacifist principles and take up again the familiar, fear-infused tools of coercion, dominating power, and even violence in pursuing the worthy goal of correcting injustices and ending exploitation of the vulnerable. Couldn't the worthy end we are seeking justify the means? Wouldn't the seemingly quicker and externally more noticeable outcomes from these fear-infused tools prove superior? No. Experience teaches otherwise. The end we are pursuing might indeed be worthy and a temporary result achieved more quickly, but LOVE-empowered nonviolent engagement remains the only meaningful and lasting way to transform injustice and exploitation.

> LOVE-empowered, diplomatic engagement remains the only meaningful and lasting way to transform injustice and exploitation.

Fear-infused actions sow seeds of destructiveness. The dominating and coercive behaviors required for imposing our will can quickly devolve into violence, sparking reciprocal and retaliatory reactions. These magnify the level of fear and multiply its destructiveness. Even if some particular injustices were corrected with coercive strategies, the benefits from their correction would typically be offset by the creation of new injustices imposed upon or transferred to other parties. "Robbing Peter to pay Paul" can never be a permanent solution.

There may be times when societal structures need to be torn down so new and better structures can take their place, but tearing down one group of individuals to build up another group only shifts the location of injustice and creates new aggrieved parties. LOVE reminds us that each individual is important. True and lasting justice requires reflecting upon and balancing the needs and interests of all parties in formulating collaborative solutions. True justice builds up everyone.

> True and lasting justice requires reflecting upon and balancing the needs and interests of all parties in formulating collaborative solutions. True justice builds up everyone.

Taking our cue from LOVE, our serving love responses work toward building up and encouraging everyone around us. When we rest in the security of grace-filled LOVE, we free ourselves from the guardedness that would view others as rivals or threats to our own security. We lose the compulsion to look diligently for faults in others so we can gain ammunition to use against them. We do not have to tear others down with fruitless efforts to build ourselves up at their expense or to bring them down to our level.

The freedom found within LOVE refocuses our vision toward those things that are honorable, just, and praiseworthy in others (see Phil. 4:8). LOVE gives us opportunity for building up others willingly, genuinely, and even joyfully—without the restricting concern that our efforts on their behalf will somehow diminish or threaten our own standing. This shifting from the more familiar and competitive patterns of human relating might initially be met with skepticism from others, but our serving love responses continuously communicate a disarming openness and trustworthiness. This change encourages a reciprocating trust within the recipients, making possible deeper, more trusting relationships and bringing about new opportunities for building up everyone involved.

Seeing and Responding Differently

Serving love responses certainly reflect LOVE's transforming presence in our lives, but our exercise of these responses also prompts a qualitative change in our perception of both the world around us and the individual people in it. When we recognize our own vulnerability, brokenness, and dependence upon this gracing LOVE, we see each individual differently and treat each one differently. Our tone toward others softens, and our actions become gentler and kinder—in a manner akin to the way our natural nurturing instincts and behaviors are brought out in the presence of a newborn child. In this transformation, we lean away from impatience and a critical spirit in our interactions and choose instead responses communicating genuine patience and compassion. We give our own gracing love with full appreciation that each one of us needs all the grace that can be supplied.

> We give our own gracing love with full appreciation that each one of us needs all the grace that can be supplied.

Although the benefit to the direct recipients of this gracing stance might be obvious (who would not like to experience gracing words and actions?), the widening circle of this grace extends far beyond those who directly receive it. Grace gives again and again and again. The one experiencing our gracing action can pass it on to others or reciprocate and return a similar grace to us.

Our gracing actions directed toward others can also work a gracing change within us. How many of us are even harder on ourselves with our self-criticisms than we would ever be toward others? We may find that serving love responses of kindness, patience, and compassion we express toward others also help us extend more of that same grace to ourselves. When our love-inspired motivation is to "give so we can give again" (as opposed to the grace-disrupting "give so we can get" mentality), there are no limits upon this healing cycle of grace. We can continue the dance of giving, receiving, and giving again with trust through every challenge and circumstance.

The movement toward kindness, patience, mercy, and compassion found in serving love is indeed therapeutic and healing within every relationship it touches. It would be hard to overstate the calming and restorative effects it brings as we extend this gift to others and apply it to ourselves. This response of love defuses conflict on multiple levels, sowing peace because it addresses the real sources of conflict.

Unlike the common, easy, and convenient approach of blaming the other party for initiating and perpetuating conflict, the honest transparency of serving love acknowledges that much of the conflict we might experience with the world "out there" is really the result of unresolved conflicts we are carrying within ourselves. Serving love's honesty also recognizes our personal capacity for allowing a fear-fueled dominating, grasping, truth-defying, and controlling spirit within ourselves to pick fights; magnify competitions; and manufacture win-lose confrontations. These expressions of destructive fear are the likely source for our own contribution to any conflict.

When grace-filled LOVE flows through us in our vulnerable responses of serving love, this fear-fueled, relationally destructive spirit is disarmed. We no longer have a need for being in charge, managing our understanding of "truth," tightly grasping our "possessions," or exercising dominating power. Would this not free us from the very things that would support and encourage our own contribution to any potential conflict?

An equally significant peace-promoting gift of serving love is a transforming shift in our perception and understanding of the other party. As we acknowledge that we ourselves are vulnerable to becoming subjects of a fear-fueled, relationally destructive spirit, LOVE evokes within us an empathic sensitivity to these same susceptibilities in others. This LOVE-assisted empathy helps us reframe our own perspective and separate our understanding of the personhood of the other party from their own conflict-promoting actions. This frees us to see them as persons (like us), needing the same gracing LOVE we continue to need for healing and release.

> LOVE-assisted empathy frees us to see others as persons, like us, needing the same gracing LOVE we continue to need for healing and release.

As we make this shift, our awareness of their vulnerability draws out our own renewing responses of serving love. We embody grace to them as a genuine expression of our recognition of the pressures driving them toward conflict and our hope that we can meet their deeper—and often unspoken— need as grace-filled LOVE flows through us. The kindness and grace within our empathic response makes us less threatening to the other party and may give them the space they need for stepping back and de-escalating the conflict.

Our action also invites them away from competitive one-upmanship and toward collaborative solution. This confirms the wisdom of Jesus' imperative to "love your enemies and pray for those who persecute you" (see Matt. 5:44). Whether we are looking at relationships on the personal level or relations between nations on the international stage, when we can humanize our "enemy" and respond to them with love, we multiply the prospects for an authentic and lasting peace. Although no one would suggest that all conflict could be eliminated with this stance of grace (genuine grace will never compel the other party to participate), grace does provide the conditions where healing collaboration is made possible.

Closely connected and freely flowing from this empathic orientation is a welcoming spirit of hospitality. Hospitality reflects the open-ended welcome of LOVE and intentionally creates space for ever-growing trust-filled relationships. We see this welcome in Jesus' welcome of children and his kind attentiveness to those on the margins of society. With this LOVE-infused hospitality, we make ourselves available for meeting the needs of others and express a corresponding willingness to receive the gifts they offer to us. It is one more expression of the LOVE-inspired dance of giving, receiving, and giving again with trust.

Inhospitality's fear-filled reactiveness puts up walls and continually narrows the criteria for relationship. In contrast, our serving love responses of hospitality remove barriers, opening new avenues of relationship in an ever-expanding pool of grace and community. Welcoming diversity, difference, and the creative spirit, hospitality sees the whole of creation through eyes of LOVE-filled grace as it echoes again the assessment made by the Giving Creator in the words of Genesis: "God saw everything that he had made, and indeed it was very good" (see 1:31a).

Our serving love responses embody a completion of the gracing cycle, but they also initiate and perpetuate its life-giving dance into the future. In the ever-giving vastness of LOVE, serving leads forward into trustful submission, *transparent revealing*, *grateful giving*, and once again into *sacrificial service*. This dance disarms and transforms destructive fear in all its relationally hurtful expressions and brings spiritual recovery and renewal, authentic living, and truly life-giving eternal life. This ongoing journey of faith is put within Christian context in the New Testament epistle of Titus.

> For we ourselves were once foolish, disobedient, led astray, slaves to various passions and pleasures, passing our days in malice and envy, despicable, hating one another. But when the goodness and loving kindness of God our Savior appeared, he saved us, not because of any works of righteousness that we had done, but according to his mercy, through the water of rebirth and renewal by the Holy Spirit. This Spirit he poured out on us richly through Jesus Christ our Savior, so that, having been justified by his grace, we might become heirs according to the hope of eternal life. (3:3-7).

Whether we frame our understanding from this Christian context or incorporate some other framework of faith, this message of a gracing LOVE that transforms destructive fear is truly gospel—good news. This news is—as a preacher friend once said—the "bestest" news we could ever hear and believe. Are we willing to trust LOVE to help us believe, respond, and love?

Questions for Reflection

1. What inhibits your living out a more vulnerable trust? What fears hold you back?
2. Tell about a time when you truly gave of yourself and received more than you gave in return. What feelings did this stir up in you then? What does this recollection stir up in you now?
3. How might a serving love response shift the dynamics in a personal relationship or conflict in your own life? How might the changing within you bring a change in the situation?
4. What might be the effect of a kinder and more gracing self-assessment of your past and present self? How might it change the way you engage with your own future and your future relationships?

Conclusion

When We Lose Our Way—Again

Is LOVE really boundless? What happens when we forget this gracing LOVE and let destructive fear draw us back into its hurtful web? What happens when our best intentions get corrupted, our thinking gets distorted, and we turn back again and again to the dominating, grasping, lying, and controlling actions we meant to leave behind? Is LOVE truly willing and able to pick us up and grace us back into LOVE's healing again, and again, and again?

Simon Peter's story after Jesus' resurrection provides a grace-filled answer to these questions.

Simon Peter and Restoring Grace
(John 21:12, 15-19)

Jesus said to them, "Come and have breakfast."

When they had finished breakfast, Jesus said to Simon Peter, "Simon son of John, do you love me more than these?" He said to him, "Yes, Lord; you know that I love you." Jesus said to him, "Feed my lambs." A second time he said to him, "Simon son of John, do you love me?" He said to him, "Yes, Lord; you know that I love you." Jesus said to him, "Tend my sheep." He said to him the third time, "Simon son of John, do you love me?" Peter felt hurt because he said to him the third time, "Do you love me?" And he said to him, "Lord, you know everything; you know that I love you." Jesus said to him, "Feed my sheep. Very truly, I tell you, when you were younger, you used to fasten your own belt and to go wherever you wished. But when you grow old, you will stretch out your hands, and someone else will fasten a belt around you and take you where you do not wish to go." (He said this to indicate the kind of death by which he would glorify God.) After this he said to him, "Follow me."

Simon Peter was an early follower of Jesus. Jesus said, "Follow me" and Simon left his fishing nets to join Jesus in his ministry. As one of Jesus' inner circle of disciples, he observed the blind receiving sight, the lame walking, and the dead given new life. He listened as Jesus taught with authority.

When other followers began leaving Jesus in droves, it was Simon who spoke for the ones who remained: "Lord, to whom can we go? You have the words of eternal life" (see John 6:68). He was also the disciple to step out of the boat and walk on the water toward Jesus (see Matt. 14:28-32) and he was the first of the disciples to verbalize that Jesus was the promised messiah (Matt. 16:16). When Jesus was being transfigured on the mountain, Simon Peter was one of the only three disciples who experienced this vision of glory (see Matt. 17:1-13).

Just as prominent were his failures. After taking that step on the water, he took his eyes off Jesus, looked instead at the wind, began to sink, and had to be rescued by Jesus. Immediately after Simon had declared Jesus as the promised messiah, Jesus rebuked him for refusing to see the possibility that Jesus would be a suffering messiah. During the transfiguration experience, Simon Peter misinterpreted the event and started making plans to freeze the moment and stay on the mountain of glory. Despite all these missteps, he continued to experience the gracing LOVE of Jesus. Even when Jesus upbraided him for his lack in faith and understanding, he still knew Jesus saw more in him than he could see in himself.

None of this could prepare him for his failure and betrayal when Jesus went to the cross. Prior to Jesus' arrest, Simon Peter had boldly disputed Jesus' prediction that all the disciples would fall away. Even if others did, he would not! Jesus knew better. "Truly, I tell you, this very night, before the cock crows, you will deny me three times" (Matt. 26:34). To this, Simon upped the ante, declaring his brave willingness to die with Jesus (v. 35).

Regrettably, his actions did not match his confident words. When Jesus needed prayer support in the Garden of Gethsemane, Simon slept. After Jesus was arrested, Simon had three opportunities to claim his relationship with Jesus. Three times he denied even knowing Jesus.

Immediately a cock crowed. Hearing this sound, Simon Peter remembered Jesus' words and was filled with shame, guilt, and bitter tears (see Matt. 26:69-75). While earlier missteps might have been attributable to excesses in impulsiveness or ignorance, this was a failure of will and a seemingly unforgivable betrayal of the promised messiah. Simon Peter's arrogant confidence was shattered, his cowardice and unfaithfulness exposed, and his personal sense of worthlessness assured. He may have desperately needed gracing LOVE, but did he have any hope of actually receiving it?

Jesus answered Simon Peter's need as he answers our own need—with proactive, gracing LOVE. As the embodiment of LOVE, Jesus' response was both tender and instructive. Without shaming or criticism, Jesus invited Simon and the other disciples to breakfast. Following the shared meal, Jesus reached out specifically to Simon. Three

Conclusion

times Jesus asked him, "Simon, do you love me?" and three times Simon affirmed that he did.

With each question and answer, Jesus drew Simon back into the community of LOVE. Proactively exercising his own vulnerable trust in Simon Peter, Jesus extended an invitation into an ever-deepening love and a lifetime of vulnerable service. From feeding baby lambs to tending and feeding the more mature members of the community, Jesus was inviting Simon Peter to follow him on the path of submitting, revealing, giving, and serving love.

This was not the path Simon had expected when he first left his fishing nets to follow Jesus. Jesus proved to be a cross-bearing, self-giving, and suffering messiah, modeling a vulnerable, trust-filled LOVE. Jesus, now personifying LOVE, was demonstrating that LOVE's focus was not on Simon Peter's past and the mistakes he had made, but on his future and the direction he would now go. With the ever-renewing gift of gracing LOVE, Simon Peter would always have a hope and a future (see Jer. 29:11).

This same gift of gracing LOVE, embodied in Jesus, is available for us all. Our brokenness, our mistakes and failures, and our bouts of foolish forgetfulness do not disqualify us for service in the gracing community nor in the wider world. LOVE can transform these seeming flaws and shortcomings into a deepened capacity for serving with grace and compassion, freeing us to extend this gift to others. Are we willing to accept this gift that looks beyond our past and the mistakes we have made, focusing on our future and the direction we can go? Are we, like Simon Peter, willing to receive this gift and give it away again and again and again?

Trusting Grace and LOVE for Life's Journey

Being human is an amazing gift, but we are not God. Fortunately, the Creator God is a God of gracing and vulnerable LOVE. As we continue on our individual journeys of faith, may we remember these truths with greater frequency. May we find spiritual recovery and authentic living in the fullness of this grace and LOVE.

Acknowledgements

I hope this book has been helpful for you. Writing about destructive fear, LOVE, and grace has given me the opportunity to put into words many thoughts and feelings that have informed my work and my living through the years. Some have been a part of me for many years; others crystalized as I was wrestling with the writing of the book. What I have come to realize, however, is that these ideas and feelings do not belong to me. They are gifts I have received from those who have touched, influenced, and enriched in my life.

I am grateful to my pastors, H. Edwin Young, Paul Duke, David George, and Steven Meriwether, who have nurtured, shaped, and challenged my faith at different places in my life journey.

I am grateful to seminary professors, David Garland, Bill Leonard, Frank Tupper, Andy Lester, and Wade Rowatt, who helped me nurture an intellectual grounding with a heartfelt faith.

I am grateful to chaplaincy mentors, Jim Pollard, Clarence Barton, Margot Hover, Jim Travis, and Lewis Lamberth, who have helped me integrate intellectual understanding with feeling awareness and deepened my capacity for healing ministry to those facing health and spiritual challenges.

I am grateful for writers who have challenged and taught me through their books. C.S. Lewis, M. Scott Peck, Richard Foster, Henri Nouwen, John Claypool, and Philip Yancey have stimulated my reflection and expanded my worldview through the years with multiple books (many read multiple times).

I could not begin to name the many other writers whose books, articles, and sermons have contributed to my understanding and whose ideas are certainly reflected in my writing. Though these sources and givers of the gifts are now lost to my memory, I am well aware of my debt to them. There are, however, three sources I can highlight that helped bring a paradigm shift in my understanding of God.

One was a sermon of Tony Campolo's, preached in the early 1980s at Southern Seminary. Another was a little book assigned in Frank Tupper's class by Arthur C. McGill, *Suffering—A Test of Theological Method*. A recent re-reading of Tupper's 1995 book, *A Scandalous Providence—The Jesus Story of the Compassion of God*, reminded me anew of my indebtedness to Dr. Tupper. Together, these connected for me that the idea of a vulnerable God of trust was not an afterthought or side issue but essential to understanding the character and essence of God. This book has been my attempt to flesh out my own understanding of that reality.

I am most recently grateful to the staff of Nurturing Faith /Good Faith Media for their work in the publishing of this book. I extend my personal thanks to Bruce Gourley, Jackie Riley, Cally Chisholm, and others who lent their wisdom and expertise to make this book better while continually extending grace to me.

Trusting Grace: The Journey from Fear to Love would not be without the many people who helped in the writing of my self-published predecessor book *Transforming FEAR with LOVE: Trusting the Gift of Grace*. My closing acknowledgement in that book reflect my awareness of their indirect impact on the writing of this one.

I am indebted to those who have encouraged and lent their wisdom to the creation of the final product. Kitty Taylor and Julia Wenzel read early stabs at initial chapters and gave encouragement and writing tips that improved the clarity of my writing going forward. Bobby Huguley, Nathan Huguley, Kim Sheehan, Peggy Ward, Brenda Vantrease, Tambi Swiney, and Julia Wenzel-Huguley read portions or completed drafts of the manuscript and made enumerable helpful suggestions for improvement. I am grateful for their willingness to share their gifts: I trust their assistance has resulted in a far better book.

Finally, I am grateful for the gift and support of my immediate family. My wife, Nancy, now adult children, Nathan and Laralee, and dog Wittle (who took supportive naps in my office where I was writing) motivated me to flesh out these ideas and encouraged me to stay on task. They helped create the safe space I needed to write.

When I consider the gift of my immediate family, my larger extended family, and the wider family of friends and acquaintances I have known through the years, I recognize that I am deeply blessed. Being human is an amazing gift!

www.ingramcontent.com/pod-product-compliance
Lightning Source LLC
Chambersburg PA
CBHW071005160426
43193CB00012B/1932